14

COMMON SENSE ABOUT THE
ARAB WORLD

COMMON SENSE ABOUT
THE ARAB WORLD

by

ERSKINE B. CHILDERS

LONDON
VICTOR GOLLANCZ LTD
1960

Printed in Great Britain by
The Camelot Press Ltd., London and Southampton

To Sonia, my wife,
and
to countless Arabs,
who have treated us as
human beings—man's
highest compliment
to man

CONTENTS

What is needed is not to broadcast comparisons to the Arab World between the merits of Western democracy, which was never practised by the West in the Near East, and Soviet tyranny, which was never experienced by the Arabs. What is needed above all is a radical psychological readjustment on the part of the West to a new dynamic Arab world which is proud and conscious of its ancient heritage, and determined to occupy once again its full place among the nations of the world.

WALID KHALIDI

FOREWORD

In a short survey, treatment in uniform depth of the distant and recent history of the entire Arab world —from Atlantic to Persian Gulf—would not be very revealing. The Middle Eastern emphasis of much of this book, however, is not intended to detract from the very great importance of the *Maghrib*, the Arab west formerly known as French North Africa. The headlines of the rest of the world have focused on the Arab Middle East; the need for understanding has been greatest in that region; the greatest dangers to international peace resulting from lack of such understanding have emanated therefrom. It is for these reasons that citizens and students of the Maghrib portion of the Arab world are asked to bear with an emphasis that cannot do justice to it.

Even within this emphasis, it must be said at the outset that the following pages are full of broad summaries of a kind inevitable in a chronology covering some 1,350 years. For those who would like to delve deeper, I have included a bibliography of works generally available in libraries or within the scope of the average pocket.

I have taken as a guiding principle that common sense about the Arab world involves, above all, understanding what legacies of the past, what current events and environmental conditions, what ideas and attitudes move *Arabs*. This book is, therefore, by no means a narrative of Western policies and predilections in the Arab world, and it assumes that these are obviously better known than are the ideas and actions of the people towards whom they were directed. For it is surely a primary need of international relations to consider each situation or issue in terms, not only of "our" view, but of the other man's as well; soberly to judge whether there is a fundamental conflict between the two; and, if there is such conflict even after such careful scrutiny, maturely to consider how it can be alleviated, accommodating both.

This seems an outrageous platitude, set out in print. But I believe it will obtrude from the following pages that our approach to the Arab world in recent decades frequently ignored the platitude. The consequences were quite as grave for our own legitimate interests in the Arab world as they were for Arabs. It is not, however, in a spirit of retrospective rancour, but of common sense for the future, that this book is written about a world of some eighty-five million human beings with whom the West must at last come to terms.

I should like to thank Dr. Walid Khalidi and the Editor of *Middle East Forum*, American University of Beirut, for permission to use the quotation from Walid Khalidi. It is impossible adequately to thank all those in the Arab world who have helped me, over several years, in research and travel. They include President Nasser, Prime Minister Kassem, and many, many others. The list ranges far and wide through many unknown Arabs who are quite as important as their famous leaders.

The responsibility for all opinions in these pages is, of course, mine alone.

E. B. C.

CHAPTER ONE

THE NATURE AND SIGNIFICANCE OF THE ARAB WORLD

THE "ARAB WORLD" is a descriptive phrase and a concept that have only recently become widely familiar outside its bounds. Why this should be so forms part of the burden of the present book. Among the reasons are not only the emergence to international view of a more pronounced "Arabism", but also the assertion of independent personality of one whole section of the Arab region formerly known as "French North Africa", and the resumption by Egypt of an active Arab role.

People who are Arabs extend from the Atlantic shores of north-west Africa to the Persian (Arab) Gulf opening on the Indian Ocean; from the interior of northern Africa to the whole southern Mediterranean shore, and to the southern border of Turkey. The Arab World embraces some 5 million square miles—one-eleventh of the earth's land area. It comprises some 85 million people—one-thirtieth of mankind.

More than half of this vast region is desert, virtually devoid of water. The more densely inhabited parts vary from rich coastland to lofty mountain chains, like the Atlas and Lebanon ranges in west and east; from wide flood-plains to closely confined valleys and belts of cultivation on the edge of desert and steppe. Such rainfall as there is occurs in winter, save for an island of summer rain in the Sahara, and another summer belt in the Yemen. Most of the Arab region comes within the climatologist's category of constant drought. In terms of water resources, there are three major zones. In northern Morocco, Algeria and Tunisia, and on the coast of Libya, the annual rainfall exceeds 25 inches. A similar zone encompasses what is often described as the "Fertile Crescent"—the crescent-shaped area embracing Israel, part of Jordan, Lebanon, Syria and part of Iraq. The last country has a dual character. Its mountainous extremities enjoy the rainfall character-istic of the "Crescent", but its great alluvial plain belongs to the third zone, since it relies for irrigation on the twin rivers Euphrates and Tigris, which are fed by rain and snow outside the Arab world, in Turkey and western Iran. It is, however, in Egypt and the Sudan that this third zone is fully exemplified : human and animal life depends on the River Nile, which originates in the high mountains of the African interior, again outside the Arab World.

The area of the Arab region, relative to its popula-tion, is deceptive. The ratio appears to indicate a very low density per square mile. Indeed, historical images, together with the desert character of much of the region, have given rise to the picture of "the Arabs" as nomads wandering through vast sands on camels, halting here and there to live in tents while their flocks graze, and drawing their water from the familiar palm-fringed oases. While this nomadic picture was at one time more generally correct, it is no longer so. Only a fraction of today's 85 million Arabs can be classified as either nomadic or semi-nomadic ; certainly no more than 10 per cent., and probably less (in many countries, statistics are still in their infancy). In the Middle

Eastern area, only 3·5 million, of some 40 million people, are either nomadic or semi-nomadic.

The great remainder, throughout the Arab world, are today settled peasants or inhabitants of towns and cities. This vast majority, moreover, is concentrated in zones of relatively high density per square mile, corresponding, quite inevitably, to the limited areas that can be cultivated either by rainfall or by river-irrigation. Such areas are exceedingly small, while in most of the Arab World the proportion of rural to urban population is very heavy. These two factors account for some of the gravest economic problems facing the Arabs—particularly when, in addition, it is noted that the populations are expanding very rapidly indeed. The familiar vicious circle of economics in underdeveloped areas is fully exemplified in the Arab world : drastically limited cultivable land ; an over-whelmingly rural, illiterate people, in many cases unskilled and ill-organized to exploit what land there is ; a rapidly growing population creating increasing demand for available food and other consumer goods, and pressing into towns ; consequent unemployment that can only be alleviated by industrialization ; low rates of capital formation, kept low by the population increase, hampering industrialization ; industrialization itself, because it is mechanized, offering only a partial solution to the labour surplus.

The problem may be illustrated by turning to the two Arab countries which are most gravely afflicted— Algeria and Egypt. In Algeria, with a population to-day of 10 million, the Arabs who make up nine-tenths of its people are increasing so rapidly that by 1980 they will reach 18 million : already some 50 per cent. of

Algerians are under twenty years of age. Seventy-five per cent. of the whole population is crowded into the north, significantly called *L'Algérie utile* by the French. Without radical reform of land tenure and massive industrialization, however, Algeria cannot properly *support* more than 3 million from its own soil.

In Egypt, the problem reaches fantastic proportions. On the map, Egypt encompasses 363,000 square miles. But a bare 14,000 of these are cultivable, and it is in and on this tiny fraction that 25 million Egyptians live—in the narrow Nile Valley to the south, and on the flat triangle of the Delta in the north, where Nile river waters can be distributed over a virtually rainless land. (By comparison, the 5 million people of Scotland inhabit twice this area.) In this cultivated and inhabited area, the soil is among the most exhaustively and intensively worked in the entire world. The Egyptian population is increasing each year by some 500,000 persons, and this increase must itself rise, as already considerable medical and hygiene programmes are reducing the early death-rate.

Similar, though less severe, characteristics occur in many other Arab countries. These pressures of poverty explain much of the turbulence of politics in the region. In view of the high rate of illiteracy—some 75 per cent. in most countries—combined with the peasant character of the populations, it might be thought that this unrest would be restricted to the agitation among only a relatively few people in the cities and towns. But neither illiteracy nor physical remoteness prevents the impact in rural districts of ideas from the world outside, and of distant political events. Radio plays a vital role in Arab politics, carrying powerful aspirations and horizons of greater prosperity to millions in remote villages. Needless to say, few individual peasant families can afford a radio set. But if there is only one set in a village—and, today, this is very generally the case—its messages radiate out to all and sundry, more especially because the Arab language is primarily an oral one, and repetition of the spoken word an almost natural attribute of those who speak it.

Another important factor in the rise of intense political action and popular unrest is the rapid urbanization, which has already been mentioned. It may not be fully realized how many Arabs live in major towns and cities. There, they are directly in contact with the flow of modern ideas from abroad. On every side they are confronted with striking, provocative comparison between the poverty of most of their compatriots and higher local and foreign standards. There have also been the pricks and darts of foreign influence and/or occupation. Again, an additional factor must be taken into account—namely, the character of the Arab family and of urbanization. Much of this relentless flow into towns and cities, as elsewhere in Afro-Asia, is not permanent urbanization in the Western sense—that is, a family moving lock, stock and barrel into a town and becoming entirely and independently urban in its roots, social relationships and standards. Much of it is, rather, a flow of individual members of rural families in search of work—of men and women who retain close and constant ties with their relatives out on the land, sending them money and frequently travelling back to their homes.

In evaluating the following short table of major Arab cities and towns, therefore, this constant flow—not only of human beings but of ideas, grievances, aspirations—must be borne in mind, for it strikingly illustrates another source of political turbulence.

MAJOR ARAB CITIES AND TOWNS

(*from west to east*)

Principal Towns			Other Towns	
Casablanca . .	700,000	(1936: 146,000)	Marrakesh .	220,000
Algiers . .	700,000		Oran . .	300,000
Tunis . . .	560,000	(1931: 313,000)	Sfax . .	65,000
Tripoli . .	140,000		Benghazi .	70,000
Cairo . . .	2,550,000	(1922: 800,000)	Port Said .	190,000
Alexandria .	1,157,000		Port Sudan .	65,000
Khartoum . .	300,000		Aleppo .	400,000
Amman . .	200,000	(1921: 20,000)	Homs . .	130,000
Beirut . .	250,000	(1922: 95,000)	Tripoli .	140,000
Damascus . .	310,000	(1922: 188,000)	Mosul .	145,000
Baghdad . .	500,000	(1922: 145,000)	Basra . .	110,000
Mecca . .	120,000		Aden . .	37,000
Riyadh . .	100,000		Kuwait .	200,000
San'a . . .	50,000		Manama .	45,000
Total	7,507,000		Total	2,097,000

TOTAL URBAN POPULATIONS ABOVE: 9,604,000

The above figures may give a somewhat different picture of the Arabs from that which has so long prevailed in the West. It will be seen that more than 10 per cent. of the total Arab-world population inhabits these cities and towns—which, it should be noted, are by no means all the urban centres in the region, but only the major ones. In some instances, the urban population is an even higher percentage of the total. Over 30 per cent. of Tunisians are urban, and 29 per cent. of all Lebanese citizens live in Beirut, Tripoli, Sidon and Zahlé alone.

What is an Arab?

It will be anticipating the course of subsequent chapters to try to answer this vital question here. But in any outline description of the Arab world, it is essential to note that it comprises very many widely varying races or historical ethnic groups. The short list is bewildering, and distinguishing "racial" definitions are themselves treacherous. From west to east, the list must include Berbers, Carthaginians, Romans, Vandals, Arabians, Turcomans, Egyptians, Nubians, Hamites, Greeks, Armenians, Circassians, Assyrians, Babylonians, Hittites, Sumerians, Kurds, Persians, and a small host of ancient migratory infusions whom it is safer to describe simply as Semitic.

In short, to attempt any racial answer to the question, "What is an Arab?" is to founder hopelessly in the waves of several thousand years of migration, invasion, and intermarriage. "Arabism" has nothing to do with "race", but with language, cultural tradition and heritage, religion (to a certain degree), and the growing sense of commonalty which these elements have engendered when fused with the Western concept of "the nation".

In general, we may say at this stage that Arabs are human beings who, in overwhelming majority, speak Arabic; who in very great measure profess the faith of Islam (but also the Christian and Jewish faiths, which does not derogate from their Arabness); who respond to the body of cultural and social influences disseminated throughout the region by the first Arab Civilization; and who today, living in ten fully sovereign countries and some thirty other territories, *feel themselves to be Arabs.*

The Significance of the Arab Region

The historic process whereby ten sovereign states, members of the United Nations, have emerged from external domination or internecine rivalry ; and whereby the impulse of Arab nationalism increasingly moves people in the remaining territories to assert their Arabism, is of particular significance to the rest of the world. In terms of numbers, the global importance of the Arab world may not be apparent. Its consequence lies, rather, in a combination of factors that can broadly be listed as communications, oil, politics and peace.

Communications

Several major axes of communication cross the Arab world by sea, land and air.

(*a*) The shortest shipping route between Europe and eastern Africa, the Indian sub-continent, South-East Asia, the Far East and Australasia cuts through the Arab world via the Suez Canal.

(*b*) Land communication between Europe and Africa proper crosses the Arab world—whether by Gibraltar, by access commencing at any point on the southern Mediterranean shore, or by Asia Minor. Future north-south railway and road axes in Africa will have their northern termini in this region.

(*c*) Two quite vital axes of air communication cross the Arab world. Air lanes between Europe and South Asia, the Far East, and Australasia in major practice transit Arab air space (though it is technically possible to make the transit via Turkey and Iran). Air access to Africa from any point in Europe or Soviet Russia involves crossing the Arab world, with Cairo as the natural "hub".

The strategic role of these great communications axes is changing as the nature of war itself changes. With the steady increase in the range of manned aircraft, the need to hold transit air bases in the region has diminished—and, in the full intercontinental Missile Age, will virtually disappear. As a result of the same military developments, the old role of the Arab Middle East as a region of land manœuvre and conquest in war has also been largely superseded. The Suez Canal now ranks among the most vulnerable targets in the world in a nuclear-missile war. Nevertheless, the Arab world will retain what might be called a major "nuisance value" in global military strategy for many years. If effective control of it is not necessary to the prosecution of future major wars, it will still be essential to prevent the effective control of it by a hostile Power.

The peace-time importance—commercial, political and cultural—of these trans-Arab axes needs no elaboration. So long as men move goods by sea, the Suez Canal will remain a vital international waterway. In the rise of Africa, uninterrupted air access will be a *sine qua non* of contact. And even the commercial route-structure of most of the world's intercontinental airlines is affected by transit conditions inside the Arab region.

Oil

In 1956, the world's proven reserves of oil were some 186,000 million barrels. Of these, at least 120,000 million barrels lay under Arab soil. Some 95 per cent. of Western Europe's oil came from the Middle East. The Suez Crisis prompted shifts in this pattern, some of which were perhaps inevitable. And as European currency convertibility increases, Arab oil is likely to meet new competition from American (i.e. Western Hemisphere) sources. Nevertheless, it is clear that Arab oil will continue as a major source of Europe's (and South Asia's) fuel and lubricant needs. By 1970, even allowing for atomic power, it is estimated that Britain's oil requirements alone will have trebled those of 1955.

Another new factor of great significance is the active exploitation by France of vast oil reserves in the Sahara—reserves which, by 1965, would make her not only self-sufficient in oil, but actually an exporter. This development has come only in the last few years, coincidentally with the decisive and final Algerian nationalist challenge. The Arab Algerians would be willing to exploit the Sahara in partnership with France; but there appears to be little hope of their agreeing to de Gaulle's terms, which now include permanent and total French control of, and physical access through northern Algeria to, these Saharan oilfields.

The Soviet Union has vast oil reserves of its own—more than sufficient, according to Soviet statements, for all foreseeable internal development. Russia, indeed, is beginning to export oil. The role of Arab oil in a global context, then, is not that of a direct clash of "oil-hunger". Nevertheless, the Western interest in an uninterrupted and economically viable flow of Arab oil has its cold-war implications. The fear of a wartime destruction of Arab oil fields, while diminishing against the likely prospect of the "swift knock-out war", will remain.

Politics

It is clear that, even in terms of communications and oil, the politics of the Arab world are of very considerable global importance. But there are wider ramifications. By virtue of its geographical position, and its contacts with both Africa and Asia proper, the region is pivotal in the development of political thought and example in Afro-Asia. Arabs have the general bonds of sympathy with Africans and Asians that were symbolized at Bandoeng in 1955. They share the general Afro-Asian awareness of a struggle to leap into the mid-twentieth century from a long sleep under external hegemony. The political, social, and economic institutions that Arabs may fashion will influence developments to their south and east, and *vice versa*.

There is, however, an even more direct Arab impact on the world beyond—through the special interest of some 220 million non-Arab Moslems in Africa, Asia and Russia. The world Islamic community is not organized as such, nor indeed is there anything closely resembling a "Church" in each predominantly Islamic country. But a generalized interest does exist among Moslems, and the very symbols of their faith direct their attention to the Arab world—to the Holy Cities in Arabia, to the ancient Islamic university of El-Azhar in Cairo, and to other peculiarly Arab foci of Moslem interest. In the wake of these common concerns, currents of political and social thought are likely to flow with increasing strength. The rise to power of Communism in any Arab country would undoubtedly exert influence in such distant places as Indonesia or Malaya. Conversely, the successful Arab development of non-Communist institutions—with or without a regenerated Islam—will have an important impact outside the Arab world.

In these, and other ways, it can be held that the future of these 85 million human beings is of distinctive importance in the wider Afro-Asian region of 800 million (excluding China).

Peace

Last but not least in this brief catalogue, little elaboration is needed, in 1960, of the statement that the Arab world is the scene of issues which were proved long ago to be capable of creating world crisis. The number of such issues may be diminishing, as once-dominant Western Powers reconsider traditional attitudes and policies towards the area. But at least four explosive or potentially explosive issues remain, any one of which could have repercussions far outside the region itself : three of them have already done so.

In the western Arab world there is the continuing problem of Algeria, which contributed massively to the death of the Fourth French Republic and which, through French foreign policy, involves the Western cold-war alliance itself. A second perilous problem is the Arab-Israeli impasse, in which all the Great Powers, the United Nations, and special international allegiances are involved on one side or the other. A third can be seen in the remaining vestiges of British hegemony, notably the South Arabian and Persian Gulf sheikhdoms and statelets (in which oil, and capital investment in London, are very profoundly implicated.) A fourth, still unfolding, issue concerns the extent to which Arab nationalist sympathies may be involved in the rising conflict of African nationalism with European Powers. Should those Powers be unable, or unwilling, to avoid the kind of naked conflict that has characterized colonial or tutelary relationships else-where in the Afro-Asian region, the very geographical position of the Arabs may prove of critical importance.

In short, peace and international stability may be repeatedly jeopardized in the future, as in the past, over issues arising in, or very closely connected with, the Arab world.

These, then, are among the concrete reasons why ideas, problems and events in this huge region need far more careful study and understanding than they have enjoyed in the past. To complete the picture, it is salutary to recall the events of the past few years, when the statesmen of the Western Powers were endeavour-ing to deal with many of the issues outlined above. The record of Western interests to be defended, and of success or failure in this effort, is a grim and be-wildering one.

It was a key interest to keep the Suez Canal open and running. Yet in November, 1956, the great water-way was blocked and brought to a standstill in direct consequence of military action by two Western Powers. This action was taken at the precise moment when the issues arising from Egypt's nationalization of the Company operating the Canal were quite clearly negotiable. It was directly against the interests, both of the West and of Egypt, that world shipping should cease to use the Canal.

It was of equal interest to the West that Arab oil should continue to flow smoothly to consumers in Western Europe. Throughout years of almost constant friction and crisis the flow had never ceased, until, again in November, 1956, pipelines from Iraqi oil-wells were blocked—similarly, in consequence of military action by two Western Powers.

Among the West's other vital concerns was the development of stable, popular, progressive and non-Communist leadership in the Arab world. Yet it is a notable fact that, between 1955 and 1959, almost every Arab régime enjoying the support of Western statesmen was basically unpopular, unstable, unprogressive. Most have since disappeared, or have been compelled to begin long-overdue internal reforms.

Allied to this general interest was that of developing Western-Arab trade, and of at least healthily counterbalancing Soviet-bloc penetration of the region by trade, aid and propaganda. Between 1955 and 1959, the largest Arab-world trading country was compelled, as a result of protracted Western economic pressure, to reorient its trade structure, 75 per cent. of which had formerly been with the West, until it had declined to some 25 per cent.—in favour of the Soviet bloc. In the same period, as a result of failure to resolve the Arab-Israeli impasse, Soviet-bloc weapons poured into the Middle East. The real and/or implied political conditions that were attached to Western, particularly American, economic aid enabled the Soviet Union to exploit its capital surpluses in economic aid for the region. And the steady development of a basic conflict between Arab nationalism and the Western Powers enabled Russia to pose as the champion of that nationalism. While some such tendency was, perhaps, inevitable in the case of Britain and France—the two erstwhile dominant Middle Eastern Powers—the non-colonialist United States was drawn into the same unfortunate position.

One fundamental cause of this evident self-destruction of Western interests was the presumed need to erect cold-war alliances in the Arab world, against the determined neutralism of its nationalist leaders. It is now a matter of history that every Western effort to cement such alliances, by treaty or quasi-treaty, failed most signally. The Baghdad Pact became a misnomer in 1958, and indeed can reasonably be held to have increased rather than reduced the danger of a Communist coup in Iraq. The Eisenhower Doctrine was, perforce, quietly abandoned in the aftermath of the Lebanese Civil War, the Iraqi Revolution, and the extreme crisis in young King Hussein's Jordan.

During these crisis-torn years, it is not inaccurate to observe that the Western Powers—and, through them, to some degree the "West" as a whole—earned the suspicion and bitter antagonism of millions of Arabs. The inspiration, learning and political convictions of a people who, for a century and a half, had continuously looked to the West were placed in jeopardy. The process was fortunately halted in time, but it has left behind a residue of misunderstanding which neither the West nor the Arabs can afford.

How did it happen? What went wrong? The answers involve examination of many terms that have become familiar in Western headlines—terms like "Arab nationalism", "neutralism", "pro-Western" and "anti-Western", "Nasserism" and 'indirect aggression". Behind these lie 1,300 years of Arab and Western history, closely intertwined.

CHAPTER TWO

THE EARLY ARAB WORLD

In A.D. 600 almost the entire shore of the Mediterranean, north, south, east and west, was held by the Byzantine-Christian Empire, ruling from Constantinople. The Empire embraced what are now Italy, Yugoslavia, Greece, Turkey, Syria, Palestine, Egypt, most of the North African coast, and a section in the very south of the Iberian (Spanish) Peninsula. The rest of the European continent was in the hands of tribes, like the Visigoths (Spain) and the Franks. To the east of present-day Turkey stood the Sassanid-Persian Empire, covering present-day Iran (Persia) and most of Iraq. The Byzantine and Sassanid Empires were growing weak, their central authority was declining, and they were exhausting each other in continuous and bitter warfare.

South of their main lines of conflict lay the Arabian Peninsula, a vast rectangle of over 1 million square miles, almost entirely desert. It had already had a strange, fascinating history—it was, indeed, almost a womb of civilizations. Over many hundreds of years, going back into the mists of human history, tribes had moved north through this wilderness, towards the richer, more fertile lands along the Mediterranean shore. Thus came the Hebrews into Palestine about 1500 B.C., and by the same route the Nabataeans emerged, to settle in the southern Negev and found their remarkable Kingdom of Petra, hewn out of rose-coloured rock in southern Jordan, where its remains can be seen today.

These historic migrations out of the Peninsula followed some of the most important trade routes of ancient times—the long caravan trek from the southern Arabian coast, notably from Yemen, up the western side of the great rectangle, and so out to the Mediterranean shore. Along this route lay many towns, among them Mecca and Medina. As spices and ivories, jewels and myrrh moved north through these towns, so ideas moved south with the handful of Christians and Jews who settled inside Arabia. Thus, Arabians living in Mecca and Medina in A.D. 600 certainly knew of the Judeo-Christian idea of one God.

But the people of Arabia were still polytheists, worshipping many gods both unseen (in the skies) and believed to live in such things as certain stones, especially the black meteorite stone in the Ka'ba sanctuary in Mecca. They were organized in blood-tribes—wandering families (several hundred strong at least), grazing their herds, raiding caravans, fighting each other in blood-feuds. Very significantly, it was language and poetry that most easily brought truces among them. At regular intervals, the tribes would assemble for poetic assemblies, at which their champion bards would declaim long, marvellously rich and colourful verses describing Arabian experience, desert scenes, love and war, superstition and question. The winner, proclaimed by common accord, would have his poem inscribed in gold on a strip of cloth, and hung in the Ka'ba sanctuary. Thus it was in the Arabic language—one of the richest oral tongues in human annals, with a wealth of imagery, and more history in its very words than most surviving tongues—that a certain force for unity existed even before the Prophet.

This was the Arab world in A.D. 610—a world entirely inside the Arabian Peninsula. But in that year a forty-year-old Arabian, Mohammad, became convinced that the truth of the existence of only one God had been revealed to him; and he took upon himself the mission of spreading this word among his kinfolk. After twelve years of scorn and no little danger, Mohammad assembled some 200 followers in Medina, whence he had journeyed from a conservative and hostile Mecca. This migration, the *Hegira*, marks the beginning of the Islamic Calendar, in A.D. 622. It was in Medina that Mohammad began to organize his followers into a community, an *umma*, of Believers, or Moslems—people who accepted Islam, or "submission" to the will of God.

We can divide this process of organizing a religious community into two parts. Considerably influenced by Judaism and Christianity, the Prophet's every saying, or observation about God and man, became part of the creed. Some of these *hadith* were written down at the time. Others were committed to memory by Arabians, whose whole minds were attuned to memorizing the spoken word, and were written down much later. The whole body of sayings was incorporated in Islam's holy book, the Kuran. The Moslem creed begins with the words, *La ilah ill' Allah*, "There is no god but God" : and it ends with the affirmation that Mohammad, the Prophet, is the "apostle" of that God.

Islam took into its creed wholesale very many of the Jewish and Christian prophets, the last of whom are Jesus and Mohammad himself. But Moslems hold that both Jesus and Mohammad were entirely human. They reject the doctrines of the Incarnation, the Crucifixion and the Resurrection—and, of course, the Trinity, since to them God is one and only. They believe in a Heaven and Hell and a Hereafter. Their God, *Allah*, has neither face nor form, and it is blasphemy to try to represent him. He is everywhere, but has no symbol. Parallels are very difficult, but it might not be entirely wrong to say that, in his mosque, the Moslem attunes himself only to the words of the Kuran which he hears declaimed—the "Word" given to Mohammad by Gabriel to dwell ever after among Moslems. There are no statues and no symbolisms like Bread and Wine, only the Ka'ba sanctuary, expediently taken over by Islam.

The Kuran is an enormous document, containing a vast number of spiritual directions and instructions to Moslems as to their conduct on earth. These can be, and have been, interpreted quite as variously as have the Christian and Jewish testaments. But the essence of being a Moslem is contained in five duties: to recite the creed; to pray five times a day; to fast from dawn to sunset during the month of Ramadan; to try to make at least one pilgrimage to Mecca in one's lifetime; and to give alms to the poor.

Islam has no Church, as such—and this brings us to the second aspect of the early organization of the community inside Arabia. Mohammad was convinced that the message revealed to him obliged him to try to spread it far and wide. In polytheistic Arabia, this simply could not be done by a handful of wandering preachers. Therefore, an organization both religious and political, and properly financed, was needed. His followers must be given rules by which to live; they must be armed to defend themselves and, if need be, to conquer in *jihad*, the holy war, those who opposed them. In A.D. 624, the Prophet led his followers into action against a Meccan caravan, winning the battle and seizing much booty. It was the beginning of a combined military, religious and political campaign that, in the next 100 years, was to take Arabians under the banner of Islam from this tiny centre in the Peninsula out over much of the known world. To be exact, 108 years after that caravan raid in Arabia, Moslem-Arab soldiers were fighting the Franks in the heart of France, having swept across all North Africa and Spain. In the far east they were beyond the Indus River in India, having conquered the whole Sassanid Empire and all but the Anatolian (present Turkey) and European territory of the Byzantines.

This expansion was surely one of the most incredible episodes in human history. It was not the expansion of a long-established, well-organized state. It was an explosion, out over millions of square miles, of a brand-new religio-political force. That force conquered all Palestine, Syria, Iraq and Egypt within only eighteen years of its foundation. It is little wonder that it convulsed the Byzantine and European world with fear.

How was such an achievement possible? Both the Byzantines and the Persians, surrounding the Arabian Peninsula, were, as we have seen, weak and declining. Inside Arabia, social and economic conditions made a wave of expansion by conquest into richer lands very desirable. The idea of one all-powerful God, who promised great rewards in Heaven for his followers, exercised considerable additional appeal among the tribes. The Arabians, moreover, used a form of warfare against which the highly organized armies they met on their way were ill-prepared. They relied on lightning-fast sweeps by light horse and camel out of the hidden reaches of the desert. The Byzantine and Persian armies were encumbered with armour, used foot-soldiers, and were accustomed to fixed battles in traditional formations.

But there was another all-important factor, one at considerable variance with the traditional Western memory of the warriors of Islam. The Arabian tribesmen were wild and fanatical in actual battle against formal armies. They were indeed fighting a "Holy War". But Islam was tolerant of civilian non-believers in the countries its warriors conquered. Moslems did not look on Christians and Jews as "pagans"—only as heretics, and minor heretics at that, for they revered many of the same great prophets. From the very beginning, Mohammad laid down these rules of tolerance. He required every non-Moslem community to recognize the suzerainty of the growing Islamic "State". But they were allowed to keep their land, *and to retain their faith*—provided they paid a special tax to the Moslem state. It was precisely this tax on non-believers that gave the Arab-Islamic state its finances, together, of course, with a levy on Moslems, and the war booty. In short, this first Arab world had a considerable vested interest in tolerating rival faiths.

This was the pattern clear across the great span of the world that became Arab—whether inside Arabia, in Jerusalem itself, or far beyond. In most instances, the tax on non-Moslems was less burdensome to the conquered people than the previous Byzantine or Persian taxes. It was, then, the combination of the strict tolerance which the conquered civilian populations experienced, and the attraction which the faith of these new masters often had for them, that greatly assisted the rapid expansion of Arab Islam.

The Seeds of Decline

The history of this Arab Empire was a curious process of growth, flourishing culture, permanent legacy—and yet almost simultaneous disintegration. The seeds of trouble were planted from the very beginning.

We have seen how, in order to spread his gospel, Mohammad organized a community, the Moslem *umma*, with himself as its head and arbitrator of all internal disputes. While continuously elaborating the religious doctrine of Islam, he also gave this community a *political* character—its rules of tolerance of non-believers, its treaties with Arabian tribes and Christian or Jewish communities, its organization of finances from tax and booty. As the Arab Empire expanded after his death in A.D. 640, it naturally expanded its political functions. Governors of provinces had to be appointed, there had to be rules for the conduct of those provinces, methods of handling finances, and lines of authority from the capital of Empire out to its most distant parts. The heads of the state, after Mohammad, were caliphs (from the Arabic word for "successor"), and they were in a sense both "kings" and "popes" (such parallels are dangerous, but perhaps worth making for broad illustration).

But Mohammad did not prescribe for his succession

before he died. As we have seen, there was no "Church" to determine the succession; nor was there any separate, political body to determine who should succeed him in temporal functions. He was not a "divine", either alive or dead; therefore there were not even the restraints such special respect for his office might have engendered. From the moment of his death, this dualistic religio-political "State" became afflicted by internal quarrels among his relatives and their descendants over this issue of the succession. The tribal, familial character of Arabian society had not been replaced by any sense of "nationhood". It was supremely natural, therefore, that this schism over succession should resolve itself into a permanent conflict between two lines of descent from Mohammad. On the one hand, there were the followers of Abu Bakr, Mohammad's father-in-law, who, by a coup, became Caliph immediately after him; on the other, the followers of Mohammad's son-in-law, Ali (for the Prophet had no male offspring). The former became known as *Sunni* Moslems (because they held that they were following the *sunna*, or "practices" of the Prophet); the latter as the *Shi'a* Moslems (from the *Shi'at Ali*, or party of Ali).

It is, perhaps, illustrative to recall what happened in Christendom. Here we can see the rise of a Church of sees and bishoprics; the separate rise of political heads of State; the rise of the Petrine theory (*episcopus episcorum*, one religious authority over others); the first Pope (Leo) securing the force of temporal law for papal decision; the assumption by emperors of religious as well as political authority; the clash between "Church and State"; a progressive solution by separation again; and a great doctrinal schism reaching its climax as this separation took full effect. There is no possible comparison with what happened in the Arab-Islamic Empire. Since there was no separate Church, from the very beginning religious symbolism and political authority were vested in one Caliph; and this dualistic state was afflicted from the outset with that greatest of all dangers for both religion and polity—who shall succeed.

Bearing these dangers in mind, what happened was fascinating and surely moving. On the one hand, the Arab Empire created a vital, all-embracing civilization. At a time when Europe was in darkness, the Arabs drew together all the inherited strands of Hellenic, Persian and other learning and art. Under the patronage of the Caliphs, huge libraries and institutions of science flourished in such far-flung, brilliant capitals as Cordoba in Spain and Baghdad in Iraq. Priceless Greek manuscripts were preserved and translated, studied and commented upon—so that when, in time, the great impulses of cultural growth passed to Christian Europe, Western scholars were able to work from Arab philosophical, political, geographic, physical, biological, medical and other texts. Among these vital legacies of the Arabs, Aristotelian thought was "saved" for, and transmitted to, the early scholars of the West. If they did no more than transmit, the early Arabs deserve a permanent place in modern history. But it was not only transmission, the mere "storage" of past learning; it was also a process of compilation, synthesis and Arab-sponsored commentary.

Over the same relatively short span of some 400 years, two permanent legacies were implanted in the

area we now know as the Arab world: the legacies of
Arabization and *Islamicization*. We can trace these
processes through the several major phases of Empire.
The first phase of expansion from Arabia brought a
relative handful of Arabians out into the new lands. As
they conquered, they established a chain of fortress
towns where their local commanders and garrisons
lived, and from which they ruled. The civilian population lived on much as before, the Arabians giving each
religious group local autonomy and allowing them to
govern themselves in great part. Thus, in this first
stage, the Arabian conquerors constituted a kind of
military aristocracy—sufficient unto themselves, pre-
serving their Arabian and new Moslem customs,
actually a minority among the "conquered".

But before very long there was inevitable change.
The fortress towns needed workers, suppliers of food,
hewers of wood, drawers of water. Around them,
therefore, grew new settlements of local people, who
came into increasing contact with the Arabians, their
Arabic tongue, their ways, their religion. Moreover,
even though the tax on non-Moslems was seldom very
severe, it increasingly encouraged conversions to Islam,
especially since the new religion was not so very far
removed from the Judeo-Christian ideal. And Islam
was an Arabic religion : its Book, its declamations, its
very spirit were Arabic. Again, the Empire was ruled
by Arabic speakers and writers. Inevitably, local
officials in contract with and directly working for these
rulers began to use the new tongue. As we have already
noted, the legal, intellectual, and scientific scholarship
of the Arab Empire was conducted very largely in the
Arabic language.

As a result, a veritable new society and culture was developed over most of the Empire, with Arabic and Islam taking permanent root. The early, distinctive Arabian aristocracy was absorbed into this society through intermarriage, conversions to Islam and the adoption of Arabic by whole populations. When it is borne in mind that the Arabs did not convert populations "by the sword"; that the vanguard which burst out of the Arabian Peninsula consisted overwhelmingly of crude, untutored warriors; and that they were almost everywhere a minority in the lands they conquered, this whole process was indeed remarkable. Egypt was conquered in A.D. 640. By the tenth century, Coptic (Christian) priests in Egypt, while still preaching their own religion, were nevertheless using Arabic in place of their own established language. The religion of the Arabs, Islam, spread out far beyond this linguistic expansion—to Indonesia—to Central Asia, northern India and Persia (whose own language survived).

Yet even as it implanted these legacies, the Arab Empire was slowly disintegrating. The schisms and factions which had begun over the original issue of the succession to Mohammad continued—but now, with millions more converts to one or other doctrine, the area of conflict was enormously enlarged. As life at the Caliph's court became heavy with luxury, and the Empire's finances suffered under mismanagement, so there arose a huge body of "working-class" Moslems in every province whose economic discontents made them susceptible to extremism. At the same time, as with many other ancient empires, the lines of communication were so long that local governors and other dignitaries soon began exercising their own authority and leading schismatic revolt. Again, the political, legal and commercial growth of the empire required ministries at the centre, and so there arose the office of Grand Vizier, supposedly obedient to the ruling Caliph, but wielding more and more personal power behind the scenes. Moreover, as the original Arabian military aristocracy declined, rulers began to think that their armies would be in safer hands if they were led by and composed of mercenaries. The Caliphs of Baghdad, therefore, turned to the Turks—people from Central Asia. Before long, a new Turkish caste had developed, called the *Mamluk*, and as the Empire grew flaccid these mercenaries began taking power themselves.

These, then, were some of the internal forces of decay and decline in the early Arab world. External forces also impinged on this world and helped to bring it to subjugation and decadence. Broadly, we can note three invasions and two incursions into the Arab-Islamic world. In 1037, whole tribes of Central Asian Turks, led by the Seljuq family, began moving into Persia and then into Iraq—following the route of those earlier Turks who had been imported into the Arab world, in much smaller numbers, as mercenaries. As the Seljuqs passed through Persia, they adopted Islam ; then they swept on to Baghdad, and spread further west into Syria and, most importantly, into Anatolia (Turkey). Even as this invasion took place from the distant east, two important incursions were made from the south. From southern Egypt, where the current dynasty was losing control, two great Arab Bedouin tribes stormed into North Africa, wrecking and pillaging all along the coast into Tunisia. Still further west, a Berber tribal movement came up from the south into (roughly) Morocco and Algeria.

These events were immediately followed by the first of the Crusades from Christian Europe, in 1096. The motives behind these armed Christian excursions to the Middle East were no "purer" than those of the Arabians in their expansion from their Peninsular homeland. There was a missionary zeal—and the longing to wrest Jerusalem from heretic hands. There was an adventurous, soldiering spirit (as there was among the Bedouin warriors of Arabia). There was a certain population pressure, as in Arabia. The European system of primogeniture had left the second and third sons of many nobles without much future ; and the manorial system of farming was slowly impoverishing France's soil. Again, just as the Prophet's warriors dreamed of earthly rewards in the form of booty and the riches of new lands, so did the Crusaders believe that Jerusalem was "the navel of the world ; the land is fruitful above others, like another paradise of delights" (Pope Urban II to the first Crusaders at Clermont).

The Crusades continued in successive waves from 1096 until 1453. But in 1206 a new, far more terrible invasion swept into the Arab world from the east—the Mongols of Genghis Khan's central Asian empire. Almost exactly 700 years ago (1258), they ravaged into Baghdad and desolated that city. Then in 1400 they swept on into Syria, ruining Damascus and other Levantine towns, destroying all forms of organized life, including the agriculture of Iraq and Syria. The Mamluks of Egypt arrested their advance. But the

Mamluks themselves were declining, both through over-taxation—of the people themselves and of their trade with Venice—and through a general weakening of the body politic because of luxury and corruption.

Stage by stage, the political remnants of the brief but flourishing Arab Empire succumbed to these internal weaknesses and external assaults. In the fourteenth century, the "Turks" began invading Europe. These were the descendants of the Seljuq Turks who, although overcome in their turn in the Arabized world, had survived as a small community in Anatolia. In 1288, a family named *Othman* had begun expanding from this tiny base. These Ottoman Turks seized Constantinople in 1453, and kept pressing into south-eastern Europe for the next 200 years.

At the beginning of the sixteenth century, the Ottomans turned their energies southward, towards the crumbling Arab scene. In 1512 they took the ruins of Damascus, and by 1517 they had seized Egypt, the key to the Arab world. Extending their hold over most of the southern Mediterranean shore and all Syria and Iraq and (nominally) Arabia, the Ottomans again pressed north. They reached the gates of Vienna in 1683, thereafter to be confronted by alarmed European defence. But in the Arab world they were masters. The Arabs date the end of their whole first epoch from 1517, when Egypt fell, and for the next three centuries the Ottoman Empire was unchallenged. Theirs was a relatively dull, unimaginative rule: Moslem, but without stimulus to that religion to change and develop; Turkish, but without making any real impression on the great legacy of Arabization.

So it was that, while they slumbered, the "Arabs"

kept their language, whether they were Moslem, Christians, or Jewish. In that Arabic language there rested a force for a new unity, and the means whereby later Arab generations could seek out the tradition of their forbears who had lived during the first "Golden Age". The language declined in vitality, but it remained the universal tongue, providing continuity with the Arab heritage and needing only a new impulse to be restored.

When this common Arab legacy has been noted, however, qualification of its role is most important. In retrospect, and for convenience, we use the word "Arab" to describe these first Arabized and Islamicized peoples. They themselves did not. "Arab", to them, meant the Bedouin, the wandering tribesmen of the desert and the fringe. There was no sense of nationhood, no feeling of national identity in those early centuries. A man belonged to Damascus, or to a town in Upper Egypt; he was a Moslem or a Christian or a Jew; he was of a certain family in which he counted hundreds, even thousands, of relatives; and he knew little more, save that his immediate neighbours spoke the same tongue. Men did not travel very far—only the Bedouin and the trade caravans. Even the factor of common language did not provide any conscious sense of unity.

It was rather that, during the centuries of Ottoman domination, these factors of common language, common customs, a largely common way of looking at life, were lying dormant, like seeds awaiting fertilization. In the same period, Western Christendom was developing its ideas and institutions, its tremendous prosperity based on global empires, its science and technology.

To no small extent, this whole process in the West was stimulated by the existence of Islam. For example, the Portuguese urge to discovery and to the development of trade in the East was partially impelled by the dream of outflanking Islam—cutting off its Eastern trade links through the Persian Gulf and Red Sea, and securing footholds in Asia from which to attack the Islamicized world in the rear. This was foremost in the mind of Prince Henry the Navigator—and of the Pope who blessed his enterprises. In this, as in so many other ways, it can be said that the course of Western civilization has been closely linked with the emergence of the Arabs ever since the seventh century A.D.

In Europe, along with power politics and rival quests for empire, the idea of the nation and the nation-state, of a "people" possessing a special identity among other identities, was also growing. And it was this idea, together with the Western concept of progress, and Western technology, that was to fertilize the Arab Empire's own legacy. This fusion of two forces, one Arab, one Western, began in the nineteenth century, as the European Powers turned their attention to the Mediterranean and the road to India.

This, the "Arab Awakening", began in Egypt, we might say, on the day in 1798 when Napoleon Bonaparte set foot on its soil.

CHAPTER THREE

THE ARAB AWAKENING

IN 1798, Napoleon landed in Egypt. His instructions were to foster a strong Egypt, friendly to France; to cut a canal through the Isthmus of Suez to the Red Sea; and to take every opportunity to drive the British out of their possessions further east.

It was the first time a European army had set foot in the Arab world since the Crusades. For Egyptians, the memory of those days had not faded: much of Alexandria still lay in ruins from the Crusader assault 600 years before. Napoleon's arrival provoked strong resistance, but Egypt was weak and decadent after centuries of Ottoman rule, and the French forces soon crushed resistance.

Within a few years, Napoleon was forced to withdraw. But he left behind a tide of unrest, a search for new vigour stimulated by the brief French administration. In 1805, religious and civil dignitaries in Egypt appealed to an Albanian merchant-soldier to take charge and end the country's anarchy. His name was Mehemet-Ali. He was not Egyptian; he could not even speak Arabic. He had come to Egypt as a conscript in the Ottoman Sultan's army. But he had already been stirred by the vision of European progress, and he was immensely ambitious. Mehemet-Ali accepted the request made of him, and began a career that was to transform Egypt.

Brutally liquidating the last of the Mamluk ruling

clique, he set up the structure of a modern State. He took over the land, and all means of distribution, in a form of "state socialism". He introduced long-staple cotton—a crop that became enormously important in Egypt's future economy. He sent Egyptians to study technical subjects at European colleges; established a printing press in Cairo; brought in French experts and advisers to build roads, irrigation systems, bridges, industries and hospitals, and to create a powerful new army and navy. By 1823, Mehemet-Ali was in a position to send Egyptian troops to Greece to help the Ottoman Sultan to quell the Greek Revolution. By 1832, his ambition was directly challenging the Sultan's authority in Syria, which he invaded with forces under the command of his son. A year later, the Sultan recognized Mehemet-Ali as Governor of Syria.

The European Powers were not indifferent to this rapid rise of Egypt. French governments continued to favour the trend—not necessarily against the Ottoman Sultan, who was still the nominal suzerain of Egypt, but certainly against any British predominance along the Nile. British statesmen, for their part, looked rather askance at Mehemet-Ali's career, for they saw the Ottoman Empire as the greatest guarantee against any Russian advance into the Mediterranean, or towards India through the Persian Gulf. Any force sapping Ottoman authority was therefore dangerous. An independent ruler in Egypt and Syria might also welcome the support of another Power—particularly France. And since British commerce was steadily increasing in the Middle East, both across the Mediterranean and from India into the Persian Gulf and Red

Sea, there was an additional reason to bolster the Ottoman Porte at Constantinople.

So Egypt came to occupy a permanent place on the map of European power politics, and her destiny was continuously shaped by these outside forces even as the work of modernization continued under Mehemet-Ali's sons and grandsons. The first major power-political reaction came in 1838 in Syria, when Mehemet-Ali demanded commercial independence of the Ottoman Empire for his own little empire. Britain was at that moment demanding special tariff benefits for her commerce in the Ottoman Empire. The clamour of her merchants for action against Mehemet-Ali combined with the concern of her statesmen over his new position astride Asia Minor. Accordingly, by means of a naval blockade, diplomatic pressure at Constantinople, and eventual bombardment and troop landings, Britain secured the exclusion of Mehemet-Ali from Syria and his containment once more in Egypt.

There followed a new and historic development. The Egyptian Khedives (rulers), pressing on with modernization, began to need foreign capital. In 1862 Mehemet-Ali's grandson, the profligate Said, raised Egypt's first public foreign loan. European banking institutions were ready and willing to speculate, but at crippling rates of discount and interest. Year by year, Egypt became ever more infested with foreign financiers, and minor but very astute speculators. When the American Civil War virtually halted the flow of cotton to Lancashire from the South, Egypt's cotton exports boomed, and her ruling élite launched out on a new wave of expansion. But the cotton boom was short-lived, and the cost of new public works had to be met by still more foreign borrowing. Egypt moved ever faster towards bankruptcy, with Europe's money-lenders and merchants clamouring for action by the Powers to secure repayment of interest and protection of their investments.

In 1869, yet another new factor focused attention on Egypt. The Suez Canal was formally opened by the Empress Eugénie. Britain was determined to gain effective control of this new and most dangerous road to India. The opportunity arose precisely through Egypt's slide into receivership, and in 1875 Disraeli made his lightning financial coup. The Khedive Ismail was in desperate straits. He needed cash immediately to repay only the most urgent fraction of his total foreign debt. Disraeli secured for Britain a 44 per cent. control of the Canal Company for £4,000,000.

As Egypt's financial straits became steadily more desperate, so there arose public discontent not only against foreign exploitation, but against the ruling clique that had opened the doors of Egypt to usury. In 1881, an Egyptian army colonel named Arabi led two revolts against the government and its foreign comptrollers. In Britain, the cry of commerce and banking, strengthened by the new imperialist intoxication, went up against him. Gladstone hesitated. He was not anxious to acquire Egypt, fearing that such a move would "hatch the egg of a North African empire". But in 1882 riots in Alexandria, in which Europeans lost their lives, forced him to act. Disembarking from the Suez Canal, a British force caught Arabi's army by night and overwhelmed it at Tel el-Kebir. Egypt's first modern and popular nationalist leader was deported. Britain announced to the Powers that she would occupy Egypt until the authority of the Khedive and the Ottoman Empire had been restored.

Seventy-four years passed, however, before the last British soldier left Egypt. Why? A general answer is that Egypt was occupied at the very moment in nineteenth-century history when European imperialism was becoming a fixed idea. Many impulses were behind it. There was the zeal of a proud and supremely self-confident culture to "civilize the barbarian", the white man's burden. There was the need of a voracious industrial revolution to find new overseas markets and sources of raw materials; the impulse of a dynamic banking world to invest in profitable new ventures; and the sheer competition that these needs produced. There arose, too, a concept of national or imperial power in which the possession of territory was almost an object in itself, leading to the race to stake vast claims in Africa. All these impulses in turn produced a new strategic map of power politics. Egypt became a pivot on that map, not only because of the road to India and the East, but now also because of Africa.

Britons in Egypt very quickly acquired what may legitimately be called "Nile psychology"—the permanent fear of an almost rainless people that someone controlling the upper banks of their river may starve them into submission. Since the dawn of civilizations the Nile had been Egypt's life-blood, and the course of events in the nineteenth century reflects her rulers' awareness of this, and the compulsive spell which the south exercised upon them.

Mehemet-Ali had reconquered the Sudan, the most vital upriver territory, early in the century. His successors had appointed British and other foreign administrators to the territory even before Egypt was occupied. In 1881 a revolt erupted there, and two years later a British force was wiped out: General Gordon was sent upriver to evacuate the area, but tried instead to pacify the rebellious tribes, and was massacred with his men at Khartoum. A wave of outrage and vengeance swept Britain, but for ten years nothing decisive was done, and in those ten years the parcelling out of the African continent among the Powers continued. In 1898 Kitchener went upriver to reconquer the Sudan, but only "in the nick of time". Belgian, Italian and French colonial expeditions into Africa were staking claims closer and closer to the Nile headwaters. Kitchener found a French expedition camped on the banks of the Nile at Fashoda, and the ensuing Anglo-French crisis was among the gravest in decades. Britain won, and the Sudan became Anglo-Egyptian territory. Gladstone's egg of North African Empire had well and truly hatched.

We may at this point form a picture of the West's "return" to the Arabized world in the nineteenth century. Seen in the broad view of history, it was a massive encroachment, expressing each of the forces in European civilization: imperial strategy and power politics; the civilizing mission; commerce and banking; the theory of modern statecraft; the West's scientific and industrial skills . . . all converging on this vast area that had lain inert for centuries. If we look across the map of the Arabized world, we see that Morocco became a French Protectorate in 1912; Algeria was under French dominance from 1830; Tunisia slid into French control—like Egypt, through usury—in 1881; what we now know as Libya was seized from the Ottoman Empire by Italy in 1911; Egypt was British from 1882, and the Sudan from 1898.

The Arabian Peninsula remained very largely outside this Western encroachment. Britain held Aden and a group of Protectorates around that vital port. Further east along the coast, and in the Persian Gulf, she had effective control over a chain of sheikhdoms and principalities through treaties with their Arabian rulers. Yemen remained independent and archaic. In the interior of the great rectangle that had given birth to Arab civilization, two tribal dynasties engaged in a struggle for control. The puritanical, fanatic Wahabi sect of Islam, led by Abdul Aziz ibn Saud, eventually won, and the united Kingdom of Saudi Arabia, which included suzerainty over Islam's holy cities of Mecca and Medina, was proclaimed in 1926.

Until World War I Arabia was nominally under the Ottoman Empire. But although the Turks seldom attempted direct rule over the inhospitable interior of the Peninsula, they remained in much closer control of the rest of the Arab east—encompassing present-day Jordan, Israel, Lebanon, Syria, and Iraq. From 1840, when Mehemet-Ali was compelled to withdraw from Syria, this whole area remained Ottoman. Inside it, the impact of the West was less direct than in Egypt, but still of the utmost significance. British commerce steadily expanded. In politics and administration, there were a series of reforms. The Ottoman Sultan at Constantinople was infected with the desire to modernize—but only, at first, in terms of military strength. Britain and France, however, repeatedly pressed the

Sultans to make reforms, because they feared that Russia might use Turkish weakness, repression and atrocity as pretexts for war and conquest. The Sultanate also came under pressure from two other sources: on the one hand from Turkish liberals and merchants; on the other from European bankers anxious to secure footholds in these vast territories. After 1870 such pressure soon came, too, from the new Germany, with its *Drang nach Osten* (drive to the East).

The result was that, from 1840 to 1914, some progress was made in the Arab East. It was not as rapid as Egypt's transformation (which her bankruptcy could not erase, however grim the resultant conditions for her people). Enough progress was made, however, to open this Arab East to the tide of new ideas from the West; and it is to the field of ideas that we must now turn in this rapid survey of the Arab awakening.

The Western Ideological Impact

So far, we have glimpsed what might be called the "tools" of modernization at work in the nineteenth-century Arab world—the skeleton of modern statecraft, the first innovations towards scientific farming and industry, public education and medicine, and so on. But what of political philosophy? Mehemet-Ali was seized with enthusiasm for the surface, functional attributes of Western society, both *per se* and to further his ambition. He forged a modern state in Egypt, but *without a nation*. He was not Egyptian; he did not speak Arabic; he was not interested in the people he ruled, as people. He built up a new ruling class which was scarcely more in contact with, or representative of, the mass of Egyptians than its predecessors. In the same general way—with the exception of one or two gifted reforming administrators—the Ottoman Turks in the Arab East ruled, but did not govern. They made tentative reforms, but scarcely because they were interested in the welfare of Arabs.

Nevertheless, once rulers began sending students to Europe; educating even a tiny fraction of the population; printing Western texts that described dynamic, vital culture and a flood of new political ideas behind it, those ideas were bound to take effect in Egypt and the Arab East. In Syria the process began in the 1830s, during the brief rule of Mehemet-Ali's son, Ibrahim, who was interested in the idea of a regenerated Arab world. He and his father were both tolerant of Christian missions, and Ibrahim encouraged them to come into Beirut and Damascus, and other Syrian towns. There were two main groups—French Jesuits, and American Protestants. The Jesuits tended to proselytize through their own language, and this in itself was tremendously valuable as their mission schools developed. But the contribution of the Americans was even more notable, because they taught and preached through Arabic. They brought in an Arabic printing press from Malta (Syrian conditions in 1830 were so backward that there was no press, and scarcely a bookshop, in the whole area), and began translating Western schoolbooks and other texts into Arabic for use in their schools. But, even more importantly, these gifted American missionaries encouraged their Arab students to study their own Arab heritage.

It was, in fact, in those early Western schools in the Levant that the long-slumbering legacy of the early Arab world, and the new fertilizing ideology of the

West, came together. Young men—not only Christian
Arabs, but also Moslems—began to examine their
past, and to study it together with a vision of the future
inspired by Europe and America. Over many centuries
the Arabic language had become dull: scholarship in
the ancient texts, and in written Arabic, had been
neglected. If Islam had been alive, this might not have
been so; but even in Islam all was decadence and
inertia. If then, we can picture a young Arab student
of Beirut in 1850 learning to read the magnificent old
Arab texts he had found buried away in old monas-
teries, reading the story of the French and American
Revolutions, and pondering the ideas of Descartes, of
Burke, of European scientists and rational thinkers . . .
if we can form this picture, we have some idea of the
meaning of these American missions in the Levant.
The same process of unfolding the past and thinking
about the future was under way in Egypt. Year by
year, more books were published in Arabic. Year by
year, the number of young men educated to the point
where they could ponder the meaning of this past,
present and future steadily increased.

They could indeed find a rich past in the first
Golden Age of the Arabs, when Cordoba was a legend
of scholarship, administration and commerce all over
Europe; when Baghdad's great libraries and institutes
were "the light of the world". The very fact of this
past now made powerful contrast with the West, and
with the state of the Arab world in the nineteenth
century. The contrast provoked a continuous, expanding enquiry in Arab minds. What was the spirit that
had moved Western peoples to such great achievements? And if they in the West did think of themselves

as "peoples", was this not important in their progress? Educated men all over the Arab world began to ponder the meaning of the French *patriotisme* and *nationalité*; the ideas behind the "American nation"; the spectacle of a newly united Italy. What was this love of country, this *national personality*? It seemed to be quite as important in Western progress as the mere building of roads, the invention of the steam engine, or even the organization of good government. And if it was so important, then a corresponding "personality" must be found for people in the Middle East. But what could this be?

These questions, this kind of reasoning, may seem strange to the Western mind. But it must be remembered that the idea of the nation-state, of a state invested with a special personality deriving from its people, and differing from other people, was then very much a Western idea. The value placed on frontiers, their role in the whole development of early Western "nationalism", had no equivalent in the Arabized world. Arabs had had neither political symbol nor a vigorous Church. They had lived unto themselves in their districts and their local religious communities— subjects of an Ottoman Empire whose rulers did not even speak their language, whose territorial divisions meant little or nothing. They had lost touch with their past. The average Briton today spends little time pondering the fact that he is "British", and what this means to him or his country. It is supremely taken for granted. In the West, we are profoundly conscious of our long and complicated heritage, and from that consciousness, and our achievements, we have developed an attitude of superiority that often makes the hesitancies and sensitivities of other peoples very irritating. Yet we are living today with the results of transmitting these ideas to Afro-Asian peoples. When Macaulay set out to give British India a British educational system, he had little idea what he had begun. Those who supported him confidently presumed that the small class of Indians going through this system would emerge as British-Indians. It was not realized that they would take only the idea, apply it to their own environment, their own awakening sense of historic personality—and arrive at the concept of an *Indian* nationalism.

Throughout the nineteenth century, this search for an identity gathered pace in the Arabized world. It was not easy. What was a nation? Was membership of it based on where you were born; where you lived; what language you spoke; or what religion you professed? We have seen how early Arab-Islamic society was a confused, dualistic one. This inherited dualism led some thinkers to equate the French idea of *nation* with the Moslem *umma*. But this *umma* embraced people as far away as Indonesia, and its symbolic head was the reactionary Turkish Sultan. Did this mean that the search should be for a regenerated *Islam*? Others rejected this idea, attracted more to Western secularism. Many of the most important political thinkers were Arab Christians, anxiously striving to find a national personality that could embrace all creeds. Not surprisingly, Christians in the Levant, the products of the Western mission schools and colleges, turned to the idea of an *Arabism* based on the common heritage and the common language of all who spoke Arabic, whatever their creed.

A Separate Egyptian Nationalism?

But even while this search was in progress, the events of the day cut into it and influenced it. After Egypt was occupied by Britain in 1882, Egyptian nationalist thinkers inevitably turned all their attentions to the enemy on the spot. Many continued to hope for help against Britain from Constantinople—especially as the twentieth century dawned, and there were stronger signs of a Young Turk liberalism in the Ottoman capital. On the other hand, in the Arab East the oppressor was the Turk himself. So it came about that a largely self-contained nationalism developed in Egypt, strongly influenced by French political ideas, and the role of French scholarship in discovering Egypt's very ancient past. Nationalists dreamed of an independent Egyptian nation after British power had been ousted. Hoping for help *from* Constantinople, they ofen disapproved of the struggle of nationalists in Beirut and Damascus *against* Constantinople.

Conversely, nationalists in the Arab East dreamed of a united independent Arab nation based on Greater Syria, in close ties with a sister-Arab state in Iraq. Thus, each group narrowed its search for a genuine personality to its concrete experience—to the confines of its present oppressors. But all were thinking, writing, talking *in Arabic*—reading the same Arabic texts, drawing on the same Arab tradition. Would the two parallel streams of thought ever coalesce, finding the greatest strength in the commonalty of the Arab heritage and language?

This was not yet a general question, in that early twentieth-century era. Indeed, when the Egyptian leader Saad Zaghloul met Arab nationalists at Paris in 1919, he told them, "Our problem is an Egyptian problem, not an Arab problem." Yet all through the period, hidden beneath the surface, it can be said that this question lay awaiting the day when Arabized peoples throughout the region, made increasingly aware of each other, could more freely think out their future. That day was not to come for many decades. What happened instead, in the Arabized world, is a grim story, but it must briefly be told.

World War I and Versailles

When the Ottoman Empire declared war against Britain and France in 1914, the Sultan sent out a call to all Moslems for loyalty in a *jihad*, or holy war. British statesmen were disturbed. This appeal might prove very powerful in providing Moslem support for the Turks, not only in the Middle East, but even in British India. At the same time, Arab nationalists sent out feelers as to British war aims. At first, Britain tried by broad, verbal assurances to persuade the Arab leaders to revolt against their Turkish rulers. But the Arabs were acutely suspicious, and sought something far more definite. In 1915, therefore, the British Government authorized Sir Henry MacMahon to negotiate a written agreement with the Arab leader, Hussein. Under the terms of this agreement, Hussein undertook to call an Arab Revolt against the Turks, with the support of British funds, arms and advisers. In return, the British Government promised in writing that, once the Turks were defeated, they would recognize one independent Arab state all over Syria (which then included Palestine, Jordan and Lebanon) and

Iraq. In 1916 the Arab Revolt began, with the advice and encouragement of a few British officers, among them "Lawrence of Arabia". From then on, some 25,000 Arab soldiers fought against the Turks, and significantly hastened Allenby's victories in Palestine and Syria.

Meanwhile other, seriously conflicting, wartime agreements were being made about the future of the Arab world. France was determined to acquire a sphere of influence in the Levant, as well as a share of Middle Eastern oil. British imperial strategists were anxious to secure the safety of the Suez Canal, the overland route between the Mediterranean coast and the Persian Gulf, and oil. The British cabinet also expected that all the victorious Powers would demand a say in the disposition of Palestine, in whose holy places so many different Churches were interested. Accordingly, early in 1916 British and French envoys signed a secret agreement to divide the eastern Arab world (outside Arabia) into two, a British and a French sphere of influence, partly under Arab suzerainty, but closely tied to the dominant Power. Palestine was to be under international administration. This document, the Sykes-Picot Agreement, was ultra-secret; but it came to light in 1917 when the new Bolshevik régime in Russia opened the Czarist Foreign Office archives and published much of their contents.

There was another new and conflicting factor. For years Zionist leaders had been working to secure a homeland in Palestine for the wandering and persecuted Jews of the world. Long before World War I, they had found enthusiastic support from many leading British statesmen; and during the war their leaders put it to Cabinet members that a vigorous, prosperous Jewish community in Palestine could be Britain's best strategic safeguard for the Suez Canal and the road to India. The Cabinet was assured that American participation in the war, and certainly American financial assistance, would be encouraged by some promise to Zionism. So in November, 1917, the Balfour Declaration was announced—stating that Britain favoured a National Home for Jews in Palestine.

Then came the Peace Settlement, the day of reckoning which, so the Arab nationalists believed, would set them on the road to independence. Egyptians had perforce taken part in hostilities; they had drawn hope from Allied wartime declarations, and from President Wilson's promises about self-determination. Britain herself had promised Egypt independence. In the Arab east there were the same hopes, based, as we have seen, on even more specific promises. In both areas, men who had adopted the West's own principles of liberty and national dignity expected with some confidence that those principles would now be applied by the Western Powers. For nationalists in imperial and colonial territories, the end of World War I was a brief period of supreme optimism, and of faith in the civilization they so much admired.

They were soon to be disillusioned. After three years of constant demonstration, riot and political tension, Britain finally agreed to end the Protectorate over Egypt. But she could not reach agreement with the nationalists about the Sudan, which they claimed, or about the forces which she insisted on keeping in Egypt to protect "imperial communications" (i.e. the Suez Canal). Egypt became an ostensibly sovereign, independent kingdom; but in fact Britain kept troops there; maintained the Condominium in the Sudan; opposed Egypt's application to join the League of Nations and virtually controlled her foreign affairs; and refused to abolish the special courts for foreigners.

In the Arab East, Mandatory rule was imposed against the clear opposition of Arab nationalists. Iraq became a British Mandate. Mr. Winston Churchill set up a curiously-shaped Amirate (Princedom) of Transjordan, under British Mandate, east of the Jordan River. France was given Mandates over both inner Syria and Lebanon. Palestine was put under British Mandate, with special provisions for the Jewish National Home—again against the total opposition of the Arabs. Only the Arabian Peninsula was left outside these imposed divisions and systems of control. Otherwise the Arab world, from the Atlantic to the Persian Gulf, emerged from World War I in the control of Great Powers. These Settlements were accomplished by main force, and they involved rebellion in Morocco in 1924; ten years of Italian repression in Libya; constant unrest in Egypt until 1923; continuous violence in Palestine after 1920; rebellion in Iraq in 1920; rebellion against the French in Syria in 1920 and again in 1925. In Arab history, the year when the Powers made their final decisions at San Remo, 1920, is known as "The Year of Catastrophe".

From 1920 to the present day, the Arab mind has been filled with a searing bitterness over the negation of the declarations of high principle, and the detailed written promises, that were made during World War I. This bitterness was to be reinforced almost year by year after 1920, until a new generation finally took matters into its own hands.

CHAPTER FOUR

ARABS IN TRANSITION, 1922-52

THE PEACE SETTLEMENTS in the Middle East were confirmed; Spanish, French and Italian subjugation of the Arab West continued. A new phase in the Arab awakening began. In retrospect, it is legitimate to view the thirty years from 1922 to 1952 as years of transition during which decisive and more dynamic new forces gathered below the existing Arab leadership. The transitional character of the period can be seen through the Great Powers' approach to the region, the nature of Arab rule and leadership in the period, and the ideas maturing in younger generations.

The Arab West (Maghrib)

West of Egypt, three Powers imposed direct colonial-type control over Morocco, Algeria, Tunisia and Libya. Modern nationalism emerged in Morocco and Tunisia rather later than in the East, and for most of this transitional period was formulating its ideals rather than actively pressing them. Earlier resistance to French control might be broadly defined as the traditional hostility of local leaders, not only to foreign occupation, but to any Sultan or other overall dignitary apparently succumbing to such foreigners. But by the 1930s the beginnings of modern nationalism were evident. There were the young men who had graduated from French schools with the classic, Western-inspired ideals of nationhood and progress; and those returning from education in the Arab East (notably in Mandated Palestinian and Egyptian institutions) with the additional inspiration of the nationalist movement which they had seen around them. Thus, for example, in 1926 nine young men met in Rabat and heard Mohammad Benounna describe the nationalist ideals and modern progress which he had studied in the Arab East. Another member of this group, which began a Moroccan nationalist movement, was Ahmed Balafrej, later to be independent Morocco's first Foreign Minister. In Tunisia a Western-inspired lawyer, Habib Bourguiba, joined with others in 1934 to form a new and more radical nationalist party, the Neo-Destour; and he was to become independent Tunisia's first President.

The years until after World War II, however, were characterized by repression and prison, or very moderate reformist demands, in the Maghrib. There was continuous inspiration from the Arab East—for example, the first Moroccan nationalist demand for total independence, in 1944, followed on events in French-Mandated Lebanon. But it was in the Arab East itself that the pace of nationalism, and the consequences of the rise of a new generation, made their greatest impact and brought the gravest international repercussions. It was not until after the end of our transition period that Maghrib nationalism broke through to the surface and, with independence in Morocco and Tunisia, began to acquire a more pronounced Arab character in direct contact with the Arab East.

The Arab East

The Peace Settlements, from Egypt eastwards, were made by the Powers without adequate regard to Arab aspirations. Strategic, commercial and cultural interests determined them. But the price which Britain and France had to pay for these ostensible advantages was very high. Their positions were not those of colonial powers, as in the Maghrib. Year after year it became more apparent that even their indirect control could be maintained only by repression. Britain had conceded the principle of an independent Egypt, but until 1936 she was unable to reconcile this with grave outstanding demands for the protection of her special interests (i.e. the Suez Canal and the Sudan). In the Arab East, Britain and France had secured indirect control by agreeing to the system of League Mandates originated by General Smuts and insisted upon by President Wilson. In the League Covenant, however, and before world opinion, these Mandates were "sacred trusts of civilization"—and they explicitly called for rapid advancement of the Mandated peoples towards complete, unconditional sovereignty.

It was generally hoped by the Mandatory Powers that the period of British and French tutelage would cultivate Arab leaders so favourable to the tutors that, when sovereignty was granted, they would willingly agree to close alliances which would still protect British and French interests. There was a slight variation between these hopes. French statesmen set out to create a truly "French-thinking" Lebanon and Syria. British officials hoped for friendly Egyptian, Sudanese, Palestinian, Transjordanian and Iraqi leaders, but did not set out to "Anglicize" Arabs. Both dreams proved illusory. The reality could, perhaps, be seen in the continuously prophetic words of the Egyptian nationalist leader, Saad Zaghloul, in 1924:

"He who holds the trust and friendship of an Eastern nation is better seated and more secure than he who establishes his rule at the points of bayonets."

Between this view, and the imposed tutelage of Mandates or the disguised protectorate in Egypt, there could be no lasting compromise. But as nationalist bitterness continued, both Britain and France tried to effect such a compromise. In the 1930s, conservative nationalists were persuaded to accept independence in Egypt, Syria and Iraq in return for treaties granting the two Powers strategic bases. These policies succeeded, partly because many nationalists felt that the treaties were less humiliating than tutelage, and partly because there was a certain fear of the growing might of Nazi Germany and Fascist Italy. But the compromises were not enough, and were profoundly unpopular among the mass of the people and all but the most conservative leaders. As a result, in World War II Britain was confronted by Egyptian opinion ranging from neutrality to pro-Axis sympathy, and by an outright revolt in Iraq. Syria and Lebanon fell under Vichy French control until their liberation in 1943. General de Gaulle's Free French Government then tried to secure for France long-term strategic and other positions in the two republics by various means, including outright force. In the end, under British and U.N. pressure, France had to yield, and in 1946 Syria and Lebanon became the first two Arab countries in modern history to be completely free of foreign rule or foreign troops. Britain emerged from World War II dominant in the Middle East, but facing another great wave of Arab expectancy, this time based on the declared moral obligations of the U.N. Charter.

The key to a new era was Egypt. But the Labour Government's negotiations with Egypt collapsed in 1946. In the same year, the problem of Palestine began to dominate the whole Middle Eastern scene, as the plight of European Jews in D.P. camps, and the reluctance of Western countries to take them in, brought a clamour for mass Jewish immigration into the Holy Land. British policy in the Middle East started to collapse amid official hesitation between the desire to reduce overseas burdens, the dilemma of responsibility in Palestine, and the continued strategic demand for those bases and transit facilities that had proved so necessary in World War II. The United States entered the scene, earning early Arab opprobrium for its support of Jewish immigration into Palestine. Before long, Western fears of the Soviet Union again brought strategic needs to the fore, and once more Britain tried to settle her differences with Arab countries by special treaty. But the new Anglo-Iraqi Treaty of early 1948—again giving Britain special R.A.F. facilities and joint-defence powers, though this time by leased bases—provoked such unrest in Iraq that it was abandoned. Two years later, the United States and Britain tried to form a Middle East Defence Organization. No Arab government would agree. The ghost of the Peace Settlement, the prophecy of Zaghloul, and mounting bitterness over Western policy in Palestine were stalking the Arab world.

Arab Leadership

So, too, was internal revolution. If Western statesmen could not understand or accept what Zaghloul meant, they also failed fully to perceive what was happening beneath the surface of Arab politics in these thirty years of transition. Quite inevitably, the period of tutelage began in each country with conservative nationalist leadership. Egypt is a good example. Here, after 1922, successive governments did have a very great measure of control over their internal affairs. Egypt was a constitutional monarchy. The symbolic Wafd nationalist party dominated the political scene, and British influence was in the wings. Increasingly, however, the King sought personal power, pomp, and private wealth. He used British support against Parliament when it suited him and Britain; he exploited nationalist sentiment against Britain when her influence seemed the greater danger. In this triangle of forces, the Wafd led the nation on the formal nationalist issues—the evacuation of British troops and the unity of the Nile Valley in a single Egyptian-Sudanese state. But the Wafd's leadership was drawn from established families whose politico-social ideas belonged to nineteenth-century Western liberalism. In general, these leaders believed in national independence; in public education, up to a point; in economic development by private enterprise. But they did not, they could not, believe in basic social reform. Thus, if they enormously expanded Egyptian industry and education, they resisted all demand for the reform and redistribution of Egypt's system of land tenure.

Much the same broad pattern developed in other countries. The nationalist leadership was in socially conservative hands, representing wealthy families, prominent landowners, conservative professionals and commercial magnates. In Iraq, where there was another increasingly self-centred monarchy, political life was so conservative that, even before the Mandate ended in 1932 (i.e. while the country was still under British supervision), land tenure became among the most feudal in the world. In Syria and Lebanon land conditions were by no means so poor, but nevertheless government was again in the hands of conservatives, and "parties" were really prominent landowner and merchant figures. Transjordan slumbered quietly as a little British protectorate on the edge of the desert, ruled by the aristocratic Amir Abdullah and his British civil and military advisers.

Much of this conservatism derived quite simply from the kind of Western influence imbibed by the men who led early twentieth-century nationalism. In effect, they were expressing concepts of society that had been dominant in the West in the nineteenth century: the power of the State in social and economic affairs should be very limited . . . indeed, ideally, it should "wither towards Utopia". But another vital influence towards reaction derived from the very fact of external domination. When a Power rules by tutelage, or exerts pressure by virtue of military occupation, local conservatism, personal ambition, and opportunism come to the surface almost automatically. The dominant Power naturally supports those "moderates" who are willing to accept its special position—and are equally willing to repress "extremist" forces. These repressed "extremists" inevitably include those who are not only demanding, in a more radical fashion, freedom from external domination, but are also in favour of internal social reform. If, in addition, there is a monarchy jealous of its pomp and privilege, and afraid of inroads on its royal purse, then yet another factor is added to

c

weigh the scales against social reform and progress. This intrinsic rise of conservative, opportunist and increasingly corrupt leadership is far more likely in the kind of evolution that took place in the Middle East than in a straightforward colony. It is precisely the obscurity of the "Mandate", tutelary and treaty-type relationship that develops this pattern. No British Colonial Office would have contemplated permitting the kind of genuine feudalism with which successive British governments were identified in the Iraq of Crown Prince Abdul-Ilah and Nuri es-Said.

The Younger Generation

Year after year, this conservatism and corruption took greater hold of Arab political life. Year after year Britain and France, and then Britain alone, seemed to be identified with it. But year after year young men (and some women) were passing through school and college, where they acquired the essential political and social ideas of the twentieth-century Western world. Thousands studied at universities in Egypt, Syria and Lebanon, and at the small college in Baghdad, as well as in the West itself. This new generation was not only impatient about the formal issues of sovereignty and national independence. It was increasingly imbued with the Western spirit of social reform—the principle that democracy involves questions of income-distribution and social welfare quite as much as formal political liberty. If it is recalled what tremendous ideas of social change were stirring the Western world between 1922 and 1952; if we imagine young men of the Arab world acquiring these ideas and then looking at their own contemporary society, it is not difficult to see the result.

The rise of powerful trade unions in America; the General Strike; the Great Depression and the New Deal; the torrent of social revolution which the depression and World War II unleashed in Britain; the Beveridge Report—all this, together with the basic technological example of the West, filtered through to new Arab generations.

Young people looked at the condition of the mass of peasants; the disease and ignorance; the inefficiency and corruption of administration; the inefficacy of parliaments apparently subject to the whims of palace, foreign embassy and conservative leadership. They became more and more convinced that the Arab world faced the necessity of *two* revolutions: one against imperialism, the other against what they called feudalism in their own society. Exaggeratedly, but not without legitimate grounds, they saw these two evils as complementary, feeding on each other. Year by year, they became more convinced that their conservative elders in office were incapable of defeating imperialism—indeed, were being used by it, sometimes willingly for the protection of vested class interests, sometimes unwillingly out of sheer weakness. To the new generation, this process became a vicious circle. How could it be broken?

Some toyed with small Communist groups. Others— and they were many—became interested in the Moslem Brotherhood, a movement of Islamic revolution that grew more violent all through the 1940s. But the great majority clung frustratedly to an inchoate middle road, watching and waiting. No party they might form could penetrate the parliaments. If, as students, they demonstrated or held protest meetings, their usual reward was police action, expulsion or prison. How, then, could this younger generation achieve revolution? As years passed without fundamental change in the pattern of power and leadership in the society they so longed to transform, this question grew more urgent.

"Free Officers"

For many young men of this educated "middle class", the Army was a fairly natural occupation. It is important to explain this, lest it should be seen only in Western terms. The officer corps of the West have a long and noble tradition behind them, deriving from an aristocratic era when titled and other highly-placed fathers bought commissions for their sons. It has been unthinkable for some 200 years that British officers should meddle in politics ("Theirs not to make reply, theirs not to reason why, theirs but to do and die"). In the Arab world, the history of the modern army is the antithesis of this spirit. Armies were the first to be affected by the zeal to modernize. To their officers, the army symbolized the whole search for a regenerated and free society. Young men became cadets because the Army was an honourable way of trying to serve this cause, a very symbol of nationalism. Under British and French influence, there was certainly an awareness that the army of a state should stand apart. But the corollary was rather different. It should stand apart so that it might serve *the people*—the great masses of the people, from whose ranks the ordinary soldier came, from whom even the young officer was removed only by a few degrees of income and education.

Thus it came about that young army officers of the new generations became more and more impatient with the same external and internal situation which their civilian counterparts also opposed. For the officers, the humiliation seemed even more direct. For much of the thirty-year period we are examining, they were either under direct British or French command, or subject to constant indirect proofs that theirs was not a free army of a free country. They were the servants of a state whose leaders, they felt, were ignoring the plight of the masses—indeed, sometimes these young officers had to crush demonstrations by their own people against evils which they themselves hated. They watched the parliaments with the same mounting frustration as young civilians, but with the significant, growing conviction that theirs was the only truly impartial force in their society, representative of and dedicated to serving the people. Only the army, they believed, had the necessary power; only in the army was there unity; only the army was untainted by personal ambition, corruption and class strife.

There arose, then, among junior officers in Egypt, Syria, Jordan and Iraq a small core of dedicated men who styled or thought of themselves as "Young Officers" or a "Free Officers' Society". There has been no parallel to this in modern Western society—with the result that when such officers broke into the news headlines, they conjured up images of "militarism" as the word is understood by Europeans, of the Western conception of "military dictatorship" . . . and even of Latin America's recurrent army coups.

A New Nationalism

Let us pause for a moment, for a summary of the ideas so far defined as being held by the restless, demanding young generation of this transition period. We have seen that its "nationalism" was twofold: not merely seeking the end of humiliating foreign ties and influences, but also seeking internal social reform against its own conservative elders who held power. The dual character of this rising movement is extremely important, because in Britain and many other long-established Western countries "nationalism" has a wholly political, external meaning. But as we have seen, in the Arab world between 1922 and 1952 it increasingly acquired a *social* character as well—the vision of "two revolutions together".

The thirty years also saw the rapid development of modern communications within the Arab world, as well as wider formal education. Newspapers, magazines, books and pamphlets, radio broadcasts and films —all in the Arabic language—increased both in quantity and quality. So too did roads, railway services, omnibus transport, intra-regional shipping and air travel. Arabic-speaking people in the different countries came into ever-greater contact with each other, both physically and mentally. In a hundred different ways, it was increasingly borne in on them that they had a great deal in common with one another—language, and the tradition it carried; the dominant religion of Islam; common enemies in the Powers; weak and reactionary leaders; poverty, disease, backwardness. Gradually, the idea of an "Arabism" spread out over the area— an uncertain idea, lacking philosophical definition, but something that touched chords of response wherever people spoke Arabic.

This sentiment was not restricted to the educated minority. The rise of radio broadcasting, Arabic films, and limited popular travel across even one frontier (for example, between Syria and Transjordan) stimulated this consciousness of an "Arabism" even among uneducated people. But the feeling was, of course, particularly strong among those who could benefit by all the new media of communication; those who had also been able to study the history of the Arab world in detail, who were under the constant influence of the Western idea of national identity. Whether they went to Western colleges and saw the product of this idea on all sides, or simply studied Western history at a distance, the general impact was the same. Year by year, the dialogue in the young Arab mind continued. What was *their* "nation"? Year by year, they were drawn closer and closer to the idea that it might embrace all people who spoke Arabic, wherever they lived. The vast majority of these young people took the *secular* Western approach to society: their search for a national personality was not primarily based on religious bonds.

When they studied the recent history of the Arab world, they saw that many of the formal frontiers inside which they lived were foreign, "imperialist" creations. Yet there were powerful vested interests in those frontiers—older nationalist politicians whose careers derived from the fact of a Syrian Republic or an Iraqi Kingdom; merchants whose very incomes came from the customs boundaries and other divisions within the Arab East. When these young educated Arabs turned to relations between the existing Arab states, they saw a pattern of rivalry and intrigue. The King of Saudi Arabia was feuding with the Hashemite dynasties in Transjordan and Iraq; Egypt's King Farouk was manœuvring between the two; Crown Prince Abdul-Ilah in Baghdad was hoping to unite the "Fertile Crescent" under Iraqi Royalty; and King Abdullah in Transjordan was also coveting Syria.

During World War II, Britain had stated her approval of the idea of closer Arab unity. But as the early post-war years went by without any change in Britain's special position inside most of the Arab States, young people increasingly presumed that Britain was interested only in an Arab unity accommodating her interests. With the conviction that *dis*unity had repeatedly made the Arabs weak and a prey to foreign pressure, a new element entered the young Arab's picture of a vicious circle. The established régimes were not interested in close Arab unity unless one or other could dominate it: Britain had a vested interest in controlling or modifying the trend in inter-Arab affairs; just as the existing régimes might use Britain or be used by her, so might they individually turn to her for help in their rivalries. Partially true, partially imagined, this equation nevertheless led to an important conclusion.

"Nationalism" thus also came to imply real Arab unity—making a trilogy of dreams: independence, social reform, unity. Young men dreamed of a time when the leadership, the spirit, the popular energies, the economic resources and the military strength of the whole region might be co-ordinated. Wherever they looked outside their own region, this seemed to be an important lesson of history. America had forged a united nation out of separate colonies-turned-states—and a nation composed of peoples who did not even have a common language and tradition behind them.

Germany had arisen from a clutter of petty principalities into one nation-state with the doctrine of a *Volk*, a people. So had Italy. And if, after 1947, young Arabs looked into Asia, they saw a united Indian Republic emerging from a subcontinent that had contained over 500 separate statelets and provinces of peoples not even speaking the same language. Further east, they saw the Republic of Indonesia striving to build "Unity in Diversity" among some 3,000 islands—again without an initial common language.

In economic affairs, the lesson seemed no less obvious. One could not study the Western world after 1922 and ignore the rising doctrine of rational use of resources within an economic region. During World War II, the whole Middle East had been organized by the Allies as one region, to ensure adequate supplies to civilian populations. This was a great precedent.

Finally, we must note one other vital idea in the young Arab mind. The Arab region had been a battlefield and diplomatic arena of Great Powers for more than a century. First there was France; then Britain; then Russia; then the Kaiser's Germany; Italy . . . World War I, and then Anglo-French rivalries in the Peace Settlement . . . the 1930s, and rival power-political designs of the Western Powers and the Nazi-Fascist Axis . . . and now, after World War II, the contest between the West and the Soviet Union. In the young Arab mind, this constant entanglement with Great Powers offered nothing but continued disaster for a backward people faced with the mountainous task of building a new society. It was not merely that Britain must be ousted from her dominating position: it was that the Arab world must be freed of, and insulated from, the clashes of *all* Great Powers. The same idea had moved young America, and was moving young India. This "neutralism" is among the most difficult things the West needed to try to understand—in respect not merely of the Arab world, but of the whole Afro-Asian area.

To many Westerners, it has seemed outrageous that any thinking human being anywhere could want to "abstain" from the great struggles of mankind—be it the struggle of World War II against fascism and Japanese militarist expansionism, or the cold war against Communism. Yet this abstention became cardinal to the young-Arab outlook. It was not an ideological abstention: it was above all a question of avoiding strategic entanglements in peacetime. The spider's web may provide a useful illustration of this view. In the Arab view, the whole area of the world to their north was covered by a gigantic web of Great Power alliance and rivalry. If one corner of a web is pulled outwards, the whole pattern moves with that corner. Increasingly, in the young-Arab mind, a single alliance with, say, Britain in any part of the Arab region was like taking one corner of the web and pinning it to the Arab world. Inevitably, the whole web would stretch southward, over the entire Arab region. It was therefore widely felt that what was needed was *united* neutralism . . . not simply in one country, but in the whole region in which Arab unity was to be forged. The Arabs, as a people, would never be safe from power-political pressure so long as a Great Power had a foothold in any part of their world.

We arrive, then, at a fairly complete picture of the four great themes of Young Arabism—the Arab nationalism of which so much was to be heard in the 1950s, as these younger generations broke to the surface of politics. These four inseparable goals were independence, social reform, Arab unity and neutralism.

The Impact of Palestine

As World War II receded, these ideas gathered strength. There followed a series of events that were to burn all of them permanently into the young Arab mind with the heat of desperate conviction and the hurt of deep humiliation. The fate of Arabs in Palestine had long concerned Arabs elsewhere in the region. When Palestine Arabs revolted against Jewish immigration in 1936, there were strikes, sympathy and protest marches, official resolutions and appeals all over the region. But in 1946 and 1947 this concern reached major proportions. The West seemed determined to impose, on what Arabs regarded as part of their homeland, an entirely new and alien society whose leaders demanded statehood. On November 29th, 1947, after resolute protests and warnings by every Arab authority inside and around Palestine, a bare two-thirds of the U.N. General Assembly voted to recommend the partition of Palestine into a Jewish and an Arab state. Violence flared up inside Palestine at once. The League of Arab States met, and decided to resist the establishment of a Jewish State, if necessary by force. By March, 1948, the Arab-Jewish fighting in Palestine had reached such proportions that the United States declared partition to be unworkable, and proposed instead a U.N. trusteeship. The Arab League accepted, though only, it stipulated, to give the U.N. time to revert to the Arab demand for a single state with guarantees for the Jewish minority. The Jewish Agency refused. On May 15th, 1948, the British Mandate ended; the State of Israel was proclaimed unilaterally; and the Arab states sent in their armies.

They were decisively defeated by a tiny but brilliantly led Jewish army, which secured 35 per cent. more territory than had been assigned to it by the defunct U.N. partition scheme. The Arab campaign was scarcely co-ordinated between the different armies. The troops had low morale. Their equipment was poor and in many instances defective, as a result of corruption in their home countries (grenades blew up in soldiers' faces and ammunition proved unusable). The fighting ended in July, 1949, with armistices arranged by the U.N. between each Arab state and the victorious new state of Israel. In the tide of fighting, over 650,000 Palestine Arab civilians were rendered homeless refugees—camped in caves, hovels and tents around the new Israeli state. Israel refused to allow them back to their homes, jobs and property, arguing against their readmission on economic and security grounds.

This defeat and humiliation in Palestine was a turning-point. It became symbolic of each of the weaknesses, each of the unrealized needs broadly outlined in this chapter. The reaction can be summarized thus: *Independence* . . . it was Britain who had issued the 1917 Balfour Declaration; Britain who had been controlling Palestine, refusing self-determination to its Arabs while Jewish immigration continued right up to 1948; and in the end, as Arabs saw it, it was Britain who simply "washed her hands" of the whole problem. *Social reform* . . . the régimes of older conservative generations had proved so weak, so corrupt, that they could not even fight their enemies. *Arab unity* . . . the whole history of Palestine, and the shameful defeat in war, exposed the rivalry of these leaders, the weakness of an "Arab nation" whose armies could not even fight together. *Neutralism* . . . not only Britain, but other Great Powers, had worked to impose Israel on Arab Palestine. The United States had strongly supported the Zionist claim and, although her Delegation had declared the U.N. scheme unworkable, had recognized the State of Israel within a few hours of its proclamation; so, too, had the Soviet Union. Israel, indeed, seemed to be a place where another corner of the Great Power web had been attached to the Arab region.

These were the broad conclusions as the full meaning of what had happened became clear. Inside the armies, the Young Officers, their reaction the most direct of all, abandoned all previous hesitation. In March, 1949, even before the armistices, there was a military *coup d'état* in Syria. But this first reaction proved only a false start, and Syria entered a long period of chronic instability.

For three more years the younger Arab generations waited, and the old pattern of decadent government, autocratic repression, Arab League rivalry and external pressure (i.e. for cold-war alliances) continued. Then, in July, 1952, there came the news of revolution in Egypt. Farouk was deposed, the old titles were abolished, social reforms were promised. The event may be described as among the most decisive in twentieth-century Arab history. Egypt was the largest, most educationally and industrially advanced country in the Middle East. The eyes of the whole region turned towards Cairo to scrutinize the new leadership.

CHAPTER FIVE

OUR ARAB MYTHS

In this narrative, we have now reached a major watershed of Western-Arab relations, and it will be well to halt the tracing of events themselves while we review the impressions of "the Arabs" that had accumulated in the West—impressions which, during the next few crucial years, were to affect the whole of Western policy towards the Arab world. In particular, the rise of a more comprehensive nationalism in a new generation, most especially after the Palestine War, raised the question: How would the Western Powers react? Two qualities would be needed in Western diplomacy: ability to understand the mind and mood of these new generations; and ability to re-examine Western interests in the Middle East and judge whether the new Arab nationalism endangered them. Looking back from 1960, it is clear that Western statesmen failed in both respects.

We shall be tracing the reasons in detail in later chapters, but it will do no harm to outline them here. First, the old habit of thinking about the Middle East in terms of force and military bases continued in Western officialdom. Equally, the profound suspicion and hostility of Arabs towards this kind of Western approach remained unabated: bayonets rather than equality and mutual trust had predominated too long. Secondly, the West's decision to permit the rise of a Jewish state in Palestine brought the need to protect that state—and this continued to cut across every possible chance of Western-Arab accord. Thirdly, the West's strategic frame of mind was reinforced by the mounting cold war with the Soviet bloc, and resulted in constant efforts to forge new treaty alliances with Arab régimes—the very régimes whose internal character was in such discredit among the new generations. But behind each of these influences against a fresh Western approach lay another, more subtle, and affecting not only statesmen, but Western public opinion. Between the Western Powers and the new Arab generations there stood a fog of fear and fallacy *about* "Arabs". Deep in the West's whole cultural heritage, and reinforced by the way it came into new contact with Arabs in the nineteenth and early twentieth centuries, there lay a body of "images" of the region and its people. They were by no means accurate images.

The Western world has had an "awareness" of the Arabs and Islam, in a deeply antipathetic way, for more than 1,200 years—a longer and more profound awareness than of any other region or culture in the world. The very institutions of medieval Western Christendom were born just as our ancestors were confronted by the rise of the Arab-Islamic Empire. The greatest chivalric poems of Europe had as their themes the Christian battle against the military danger and religious heresy of the "Mahometan" Arabs. For centuries, Western schoolchildren have read the *Chanson de Roland*. Roland's enemies are the wild, golden-armoured Saracens—though his actual enemies at Roncevalles were Christian Basque brigands. This theme of danger and religious threat was carried forward in the legends about the Crusades. In Western culture, the very concepts of valour, patriotism, honour and mission derive from and are permeated by this antipathetic attitude towards Arabs and Islam.

Even when the Arabs, as such, had faded from the picture after their conquest by the Ottoman Turks, those conquerors continued the adverse image—because they were Moslem, threatened the very heart of Europe, and did commit dreadful massacres even as late as the 1870s. The "image" Westerners had, and indeed still have deep in their subconscious, could be defined as follows: Arabs are barbaric; they are the enemies of Christianity not only because they preach a heresy, but because they kill all Christians (though, as we have seen, the early Arab Empire was in fact based on tolerance); they are the proven enemies of Europe both on these grounds and because they once battled their way into the very heart of France and, later, advanced all the way to Vienna (the Turks being confused with Arabs).

We should, of course, add to this first "image" the general reaction of Western culture to all non-white peoples. The West is supremely proud of the achievements of its own civilization. Even as pride, and faith in its capacity to progress, steadily increased, so its contacts with "backward" non-white peoples increased. This process reached the point where Westerners came to believe, very genuinely, that human beings with white skin had some innately superior ability. This racial superiority complex is still ingrained, though it is now refuted by science. We have to add it to the composite attitude that has affected the modern Western approach to Arabs.

From the nineteenth century forward, a second vital image was built up in the Western mind. It might be called the Desert-Bedu Fascination. The Bible, and early Western contacts with Arabs, gave us to understand that the people in and all around the Holy Land were wandering nomads on camels, horses and donkeys living in a wilderness of sand. And indeed, as we have seen, this was perfectly true of the early Arabs, and continued to be true of vast tracts of the Arab world well into the nineteenth century. As Western travellers, scholars and officials journeyed through the area in that century, this picture of the Arab and his world was powerfully reinforced. A whole new theme of adventure arose in Western literature—the theme of the brave Westerner who journeyed into limitless deserts, battling against a harsh sun, parched throat, mirages, and the terrible dangers of fierce Arab tribesmen swooping out of the sands. The Gordon-Kitchener episodes in the Sudan added to this theme (one has only to think of the film, *The Four Feathers*, and the innumerable stories of the Foreign Legion).

Then, as we have already noted, during World War I Britain sought out an Arabian leader, Hussein, to head the Arab Revolt against the Turk. Hussein was the scion of a great Arab aristocracy of the desert; his warriors were Bedouin. The Briton who became associated with this episode was Colonel T. E. Lawrence—"Lawrence of Arabia". His exploits were popularized all over the Western world immediately after the Great War—by lectures and film-shows, newspaper articles, books about and by him, pictures of him wearing the colourful dress of the British-Arab desert warrior, the "uncrowned King of Arabia". The mass popularization of this episode coincided with Rudolf Valentino and his sheik, in which a strange new idea was introduced: the picture of the Arab desert chieftain who is noble, dignified, lives by his own somehow admirable code of honour and chivalry, and whisks gentle (white) maidens into his sandy retreats, until they are rescued by brave (white) officers.

At much the same time, serious books on the Arab desert by Lawrence and others made a profound impression among Western intellectuals. The desert is fascinating. For the Westerner, increasingly caught up in a drab and crowded Machine Age, in the soot and pressure of industrial life, the desert is clean and exciting. It is a place where a man can breathe deeply, test himself to the utmost, and come face to face with the great Absolutes of human existence. In many respects, both for those who know it and those who can only imagine it from Western armchairs, it has a sister-fascination to that of great mountain peaks or vast oceans. But there is something more about the Arab desert. It contains people, the wandering Bedouin tribes, who seem at home in this fascinating environment. They appear to see life to a great extent in the clear absolutes of the desert itself. To the Westerner, the Bedouin seem to have few of the doubts, the fears, the reasoned uncertainties that lie at the roots of twentieth-century rationalist and materialist culture. They have a nobility of tradition; they seem to be true aristocrats, treasuring their ancestry (and in the West there is a certain yearning for such aristocracy). They have a simple religion which seems at its very finest in the desert. To many Westerners, the sight of a Bedu Arab kneeling towards an unseen Mecca, praying to a

God without face, form, church or icon, in a vast expanse of beautifully clean sand, is both troubling and enormously attractive.

So it came about that this new, somewhat *positive* Arab image entered Western culture. At the very same period of history, Western Governments were beginning the thirty transitional years of close involvement with the Arab East. Most especially for Britain, this contact was primarily *with* noble, aristocratic Arab kings and chieftains from the desert. King Abdullah was given a throne in Transjordan, and for thirty years British officials worked with him and with a Bedouin army built up into the famous Arab Legion of Glubb Pasha. In Iraq, Britain put another of Hussein's sons on a throne—King Feisal I—and worked with this dynasty as the very linch-pin of British policy in the Middle East until 1958. It was a supremely natural relationship. It expressed the Desert-Bedu Fascination; it met an instinctive British search for some tradition and aristocracy among Arabs as the "best" kind of leadership; and it was precisely what Western public opinion expected.

There was, however, another side to this powerful Arab image. There were the rapidly growing towns, cities and coastal ports of the Arab world, with which literally millions of Westerners had the greatest contact—in the armies of two world wars, the occupation and treaty-base garrisons, the travels of businessmen and tourists. Virtually everything to be seen in these *urban* Arab settings was negative and distasteful. The range of such impressions stretched all the way from the pestering souvenir- and dirty-postcard-vendors of Aden and Port Said; through the bazaars and slums, with their squalor, thievery, cunning "Oriental merchants" and dim and dubious night-haunts, to the violence of "street mobs". The sight of an Arab praying to Mecca in such surroundings evoked in the Western mind all that was negative about Islam, in contrast to the idealized picture of Islam-in-the-Desert.

Moreover, it was in the *urban* Arab world that Western culture made its impact—and much of what the average Westerner saw of the result was distasteful. Here the range of impressions was equally wide. The very rich seemed to emulate Western standards without taste or restraint. But at least they could be tolerated because they were quite obviously the "best behaved and most cultured", next to the noble houses of the desert aristocrats (who might have less formal education, but did have great dignity). Below the very rich there were the *nouveaux riches*, and below them again the commercial and professional "middle classes". The attitude of the average Briton to the last was bound to be somewhat disdainful—a carry-over from the Imperial days when the "white-collar native" was apt to be the most hostile, yet servile. It was by this middle class that the Westerner was most liable to have the moral precepts of his own civilization invoked against him, with the irritating suggestion that his Government was not exactly practising in the Arab world what it preached, and what it practised at home.

And of course it was from this stratum of urban Arab society that the "extremists" of the thirty transitional years came. They were against the aristocratic régimes which Britons admired and supported; they were against Britain; they were always "fomenting sedition and riot". In this group were the students discussed in the last chapter; the political leaders who, in opposition if not in jail, were always seen behind "the mob" (i.e. the very poor, discontented urban Arab who looked to these young generations). In short, and in broad terms, the *young urban Arab was a "bad" Arab.* His conservative elders, especially if they were from aristocratic desert stock, were "good" Arabs, to be supported and protected in the West's interests. This natural inclination increasingly matched political realities. For it was the "good" Arab who was willing to grant the Western Powers bases, and sign alliances. So it was that the "good" Arab became the "pro-Western" Arab; and all who opposed him, the "bad" ones, became "anti-Western" and very probably Communist. If there was a demonstration in Baghdad, Nuri es-Said told British authorities that it was the work of "Communists", and accordingly justified a police-state repression that became more and more all-embracing as the years went by.

Finally, we have to note two other influences in the West's accumulated ideas about the Arab world. Deep in our culture there is a profound dislike of "the Egyptian". There are many reasons. One derives from our Scriptures. Another factor is the sense of distaste which a very superior Western civilization feels for a people who, as descendants of the earliest organized society, could yet have "sunk so low" into such appalling poverty and disease. Yet another cause of this Egyptophobia lies in the variety of cultural influences that have passed into Egypt—notably the "Turkish" character of the ruling class with which Europeans had contact until the twentieth century.

The modern educated Egyptian is rather more "sophisticated" than his counterpart elsewhere in the Arab world—but in a baffling, elusive way that irritates many Westerners. In addition, a greater number of Westerners, particularly Britons, have experienced Egypt more negatively than they have other parts of the Arab world. More very ordinary Britons, as soldiers, have known danger and disease while occupying Egypt. More stories of Cyprus-style guerrilla warfare, and religious fanaticism (Egypt was the centre of the Moslem Brotherhood), have filtered back into the West from Egypt.

If, then, the word "Egyptian" strikes a particularly negative response in the Western mind, there is still another factor in Western images. The Egyptians are one of the oldest peoples on earth. Applying a profound race-consciousness, we generally presume that they are "a separate race from the Arabs" (although, as we have seen, race has nothing whatever to do with who is Arab). In culture and language, Egypt has been Arab for 1,000 years. But this conviction, that "Egypt is not Arab", has also, until recently, been stimulated by the nature of Egyptian nationalism itself, which, until the 1950s, concentrated very largely on its own particular problems with Britain inside Egypt and the Sudan.

The result of all these influences was that when the West saw a young Egyptian military officer leading an "extremist" nationalism that year by year seemed to "spread" ever more widely over the whole Arab world, one conclusion was very easy to reach. This nationalist tide must be artificial. And since the Arabs who increasingly hailed him as their leader were young urban Arabs, who opposed their elders—"bad" Arabs opposing the "good" Arabs—the broad Western conclusion was simply reinforced. When there was a demonstration against Mr. Selwyn Lloyd on his arrival at Bahrein in 1956, the British Minister was immediately assured by his own subordinates (and by elderly Bahreini Sheikhs) that it was "all the work of Nasser". It seemed to make good sense. Here was "the street Arab" (the dirty urban variety) being whipped up "artificially" by a "non-Arab" Egyptian imperialist dictator against "our friends" in Bahrein. Yet as we have seen in the preceding chapter, the movement of discontent all over the Arab world, this movement of new generations, was rising years before Gamal Abdel Nasser was heard of.

Time and again, in the rest of this narrative, these Western myths and prejudices, these fears and fallacies about "the Arabs", will be seen at work. It is not unusual for people in one region or culture-group to have erroneous ideas about another—indeed, many of the tensions of the world spring from this source. The West has had fallacious ideas about many other non-Western, "non-white" peoples, and *vice versa*. But the very significant fact is that Western "images" of the Arabs have been developing longer, more persistently, and more negatively than have their images of any other cultural group challenging the West. And at the very moment in history when the need for an accurate understanding of Arabs was greatest, new influences (like the Lawrence legend) reinforced those of earlier centuries. The very character of the régimes the Western Powers then established continued to reinforce the wrong impression.

The irony needs to be underlined. It was the West that gave "Young Arabism" much of its ideology—most especially the modern impulse to its search for nationhood, and its impatience for social reform. For thirty years, in Western universities, and in institutions in the Middle East under Western influence, these young men and women were educated towards precisely the goals which Western statesmen and their Arab "friends" increasingly denied them. Running through every crisis of the last ten years, there is this theme of irony: this inability to understand and come to terms with *urban Arab nationalism*.

To this day, the old myths continue, in their various forms—for myths of this kind are seldom consistent. Even today, if 100 average Westerners were asked, 'What is a real Arab like?", the majority answer would probably be a picture of a Bedu tribesman in his flowing white robe and traditional headdress, with a horse or camel, a rifle, and a background of sand and oasis-palms (and perhaps an oil-well). Yet of some 40,000,000 human beings in the Middle East, including the Arabian Peninsula, no more than 3,500,000 are either nomad or semi-nomad. One-fifth of the total population of the central and eastern Arab world lives in the twenty largest cities and towns alone. Nor is this some sudden development within the last few years. Urbanization has marked the development of Arab society throughout this century; so has the extension of sedentary farming communities. In Egypt, the Bedu myth has been erroneous ever since the rise of the modern state after Mehemet-Ali. (Yet in 1955 a well-educated American Navy officer, talking with an Egyptian colleague in Italy and learning that he lived in Cairo, asked him in all seriousness, "Oh? Is your tent pitched near the Nile?") In its general application, the Bedu myth can be seen in virtually every political cartoon, and in the most up-to-date children's story-books, with their tales of desert adventure.

In the same way, the ancient fears of Christendom have caused much of the West's negative reaction to "Pan-Arabism", and to that spectre of "Nasser's Empire" which in itself is so much a product of the ideas we have been tracing in this chapter. It is uncomfortable to the Western mind to think of Arabs uniting in one great movement. The words "Arab nationalism from the Atlantic to the Persian Gulf" evoke centuries-old worries, not excluding a subconscious picture of wild Moslems hacking off Christian heads with curved scimitars. A *Life* magazine article in 1958, about "Nasser's bid for empire", was illustrated by a huge full-page photograph of him speaking into microphones before a big flag that bore a curved sword. The caption read, "*Under Banner bearing Sword of Islam, Gamal Abdel Nasser exalts the Glories of the United Arab Republic*". (The caption was particularly inapt: the U.A.R. has the first secular constitution in the Arab world; the flag in question was that of Yemen.)

It is important, then, in viewing the recent history of conflict between the Arabs and the West, to bear these cultural influences, these fearful and erroneous images, in mind. The idea that all Arabs are nomads of the desert was subtly transformed into the conviction that all "good" Arabs are of desert aristocracy. The Bedu-desert fixation helped to blind the West to the rise of a vigorous new urban generation expressing a comprehensive *urban* Arab nationalism, against their aristocratic and conservative elders, and against the Western Powers. Because Western statesmen sought strategic bases, and were able to get them from the older aristocracy; because younger Arabs opposed such alliances; because their leader was "not an Arab" in Western eyes, Western policies moved rapidly towards disaster. This grim process lasted until the day in 1958 when all "our friends" were dead, overthrown by revolution, or being protected from popular anger by Western fleets and paratroopers. As the West began to recover from this shock, a genuine Communist drive began in the very Arab country on whose feudal-aristocratic régime this body of myths and obsolete assumptions had been most rigidly focused.

CHAPTER SIX

YOUNG ARABISM IN REVOLT

IT WAS NOT UNTIL three years after the "last straw" of Palestine that what we may conveniently call "Young Arabism" won power in any country. On July 26th, 1952, after a bloodless revolution, King Farouk sailed away into exile, and young Army officers began trying to consolidate the historic change in Egypt. They had been led throughout by Colonel Gamal Abdel Nasser. The Free Officers, however, made General Neguib their public leader—an older man who had had no part in their years of secret planning, but whose maturity, it was hoped, would reassure commerce and educated Egyptians.

Immediately after the successful coup, the question arose: What form of government for Egypt? Colonel Nasser argued—against the initial opposition of his fellow-officers—in favour of trying to restore parliamentary democracy. The officers finally agreed, and he asked the Wafd Party to form a government, on condition that they would pass basic reforms, particularly land reform. The Wafd refused, thereby beginning Nasser's doubts about any early introduction of Western-style democracy for Egypt. Neguib was made Prime Minister. Land reform was decreed. Throughout 1953 and 1954, revolutionary Egypt was seized of crisis after crisis as various groups—the Moslem Brotherhood, the Communists, the parties of the *ancien régime*—tried to take power. Elections were postponed. The young officers, who had presumed that the Army's role would be entirely that of caretaker, increasingly came to the conviction that they could not withdraw from politics. General Neguib was enormously popular as a father-figure of the Revolution. But as the political instability continued, he began demanding full powers for himself—whereas the younger officers had always regarded him as a leader among them. The final clash came, and they deposed him. Nasser became Prime Minister.

Throughout this period, Arab nationalists watched Egypt closely, by no means certain what kind of revolution this was, or what manner of leadership would finally emerge. The interest was intense and continuous, for Egypt was the largest, most advanced country at the centre of the Arab world, as well as the Arabic cultural centre, and the first to revolt against decadent, reactionary government. What would the new Egypt do in external affairs? There were four major questions: the evacuation of British troops; the future of the Sudan; Egypt's role in the Arab world; and her relations with the Great Powers. In a very real sense, nationalists began "testing" Egypt on these issues—as well, of course, as her officers' evident concern for social reforms.

Agreement came first on the Sudan, when the revolutionary Government proposed to Britain that the Sudanese should have the right to choose between union with Egypt or independence. Britain agreed, and the process of Sudanese self-government accelerated. But the classic anxiety of Egypt towards the territory lying astride her life-blood—the Nile waters —reappeared in the form of considerable interference in the Sudan. The Sudanese Parliament finally opted for independence, however, and Egypt accepted.

The Anglo-Egyptian agreement about the Sudan paved the way for talks on evacuation, the most thorny subject of all. In the minds of Western statesmen, this issue was wholly bound up with the strategic problems of the cold war. In 1953, before the evacuation agreement, U.S. Secretary Dulles visited Cairo for talks with the revolutionary régime (which America had initially welcomed). To Colonel Nasser, he propounded the need for a new Middle East defence alliance, and in this and many other minor ways suggested that, in return, America would press Britain to withdraw from Egypt. Nasser replied that he opposed all alliances between Great Powers and any part of the Arab world. Elaborating, he asked what use "linear strategy" and external alliance would be when the real danger was from "an attack from inside"? He told the American Secretary that sound defences of the Arab world against external domination must be found in "a force that could bind Arabs together" as they built a modern society—the force of nationalism. Mr. Dulles went away unconvinced and disappointed, but continued to exert pressure on Britain to sign an evacuation accord.

Agreement was finally reached in 1954. It included an Egyptian compromise allowing British civilians to maintain the great Canal Zone base for seven years, and provided for British re-entry should Turkey, or any Arab League state, be attacked by an outside Power. Signing this very unpopular compromise (after seventy-two years, compromise with Britain was bound to be unpopular), Nasser publicly stressed that Egypt was neutralist in peacetime and opposed all non-Arab alliances. But his policy was unproven. The Moslem Brotherhood seized on the unpopular agreement. In the summer of 1954, after repeated incidents, including an attempted assassination of Nasser at a public rally in Alexandria, the Brotherhood was completely repressed.

It was in this same year of 1954 that evidence of a new determination among Arab nationalists could be seen throughout the region. Resistance to French rule in Morocco steadily increased. Similar action in Tunisia persuaded M. Mendès-France to negotiate with Tunisians for home rule. In November, 1954, the historic nationalist rebellion in Algeria began. Egypt showed strong sympathy with these tensions in the Arab West, and in May, 1954, nationalists of the three North African countries formed a Liberation Committee in Cairo. Further east, in Jordan, there was evidence of stronger pressure against the old political order sponsored by Britain. The entire character of Jordanian politics had changed since 1949, when the "West Bank" remnant of Palestine (i.e. the territory lying between Israel's eastern armistice line and the River Jordan) had been annexed to the former Transjordan. Two-thirds of the population were now Palestine Arabs—half of these refugees, but with votes—expressing urban Arab nationalism. The carefully organized general election of 1954, designed to conceal the demands of this restless majority, was symptomatic.

In Syria, in September, 1954, elections returned to Parliament a significant number of deputies of the Ba'ath Party—formed by Western-educated intellectuals and politicians who espoused neutralism, socialism and urgent and close Arab unity. In Iraq, Nuri es-Said deemed it advisable to dissolve all party-political groups, and to suspend a Parliament which had itself been hand-picked to preserve the existing order.

In summary, it must be observed that in 1954, while Colonel Nasser had yet to emerge as the leader and popular symbol of the Young Arabism we have been examining, there was clear evidence of its growing strength in each critical area of the Arab world. If nationalism in the *Maghrib* (Arab West), was less Pan-Arab than in the Middle East, it was nevertheless clear that there, too, a new and more intensive phase had been reached, inspiring and being inspired by events in the centre and east.

The Western Powers, however, were preoccupied with a different approach to the problems of the region. The termination of the war in Indo-China, and the last-resort solution evolved at Geneva, initiated a new phase in the policy of cold-war "containment". It became a primary objective to link N.A.T.O. in Europe with the Western Powers' strategic positions in Asia—in Japan, the Philippines, and Australasia. Mr. Dulles pressed for the organisation of S.E.A.T.O. (South East Asia Treaty Organization), to which Pakistan, already receiving U.S. military aid, at once adhered. There remained the presumed need to complete this strategic network between Pakistan and Turkey (in N.A.T.O.), and in the Middle East. By the end of 1954, Turkey and Pakistan had concluded a treaty, and Iraq had signed a military aid agreement with the United States. It was held desirable to extend the treaty network to Iraq and its vital oilfields, with the further hope that Iraqi membership might induce wider Arab participation.

In retrospect, then—for the point was manifestly not appreciated at the time—the three Western Powers were confronted at the end of 1954 with decisions likely to affect Western-Arab relations for many years. There was clear evidence, if statesmen were capable of perceiving it, that the entire political order in the Arab world was undergoing new stress from below. At the centre, in Egypt, a revolutionary leadership had concluded agreements with Britain that left the way open for better relations—but subject to Egyptian attitudes of which there could be no serious doubt. If officials in London were inclined to question the strength of Premier Nasser's neutralist professions, the events of 1954 strongly suggested that his Government would not in any case *survive* any non-neutralist policy. In the Arab West, nationalism was openly challenging French power in all three territories. In the Arab East the traditional pivot of British policy, the régime of Nuri es-Said, was manifestly unpopular even without any new alliances with Western Powers.

It was necessary to consider, then, whether Western interests would be advanced, or jeopardized, by pressing new alliances into a region where the existing ones were so clearly unpopular. It could be held that the interests of the Western Powers demanded the most profound re-examination of their whole traditional role in the region, and demanded the utmost probing of the ideas and predilections of a new generation whose emergence to power had already begun. The need for such reappraisal would have existed quite independently of any special Soviet interest in the

Arab world. The mounting evidence of such Soviet interest underlined the question whether any Western alliance was calculably worth maintaining by means of unpopular Arab régimes.

In the event, it was a French Government, led by M. Mendès-France, that did produce a partial answer to these questions in the case of Morocco and Tunisia; only to suffer defeat over the public reaction to what was described as a policy of "abandonment" in North Africa following "scuttling" in Indo-China. In 1956, this reaction was to produce grave repercussions, via Algeria, in the rest of the Arab world.

Neither the U.S. nor British Governments proved capable of meeting the new challenges. The first clear evidence of this failure came early in 1955, in the formation of the Baghdad Pact.

The Baghdad Pact

In December, 1954, Nuri es-Said announced that he would not sign any new, non-Arab alliance without first consulting the other members of the Arab League defence pact. In January, 1955, however, he did initial such an alliance with the Prime Minister of Turkey— the Turco-Iraqi Pact that was the beginning of the Baghdad Pact (for mutual, manifestly anti-Soviet defence), later to include Iran, Pakistan, and Britain. Britain at once indicated approval. Four days later, Egypt launched a vociferous propaganda assault against Nuri and the British Government. In the separate reactions to this Egyptian campaign, of Arabs on the one hand and the West on the other, there could be seen the whole chasm of misunderstanding. Premier Nasser's outspoken opposition to the Baghdad Pact

D

was, in a very real sense, the first major "proof" of his stature as the kind of leader for whom Young Arabism had been waiting. From that moment, his prestige rapidly increased until he became a symbol of this rising generation. In opposing the new, Baghdad-based alliance, Nasser did not create a new Arab attitude, but merely expressed one long ante-dating his emergence to power.

In the West, however, there was anger and indignation. What to Arab nationalists appeared as the resumption by Egypt of her full place in the Arab world was interpreted in the West as the nascent imperialism of a "non-Arab" military dictator who needed a foreign diversion to control a restless Egypt. There was anger in Britain because, in addition, it was felt that she had "done Nasser a good turn" by agreeing to evacuate the Suez Canal Zone. So wide was the gap between prevailing Western ideas and Arab-world realities that it was almost expected that the 1954 Evacuation Agreement should earn the unquestioning gratitude of the Egyptian Government. Certainly, it was felt to be intolerable that such a Government should now attack British policy in Arab countries in which Egypt allegedly had no legitimate concern.

The Baghdad Pact was formally inaugurated on February 24th, 1955. Four days later there occurred a second historic event. In what her Government described as a reprisal for trans-border raids, Israeli military forces heavily attacked Gaza—which contained some 200,000 Palestine Arab refugees—with considerable loss of Egyptian life. This "Gaza Raid" was the gravest Arab-Israeli incident since 1949. The Egyptian revolutionary régime had until then evinced signs of—at the least—wishing to reduce Arab-Israeli tension. While it continued this policy along the Egyptian-Israeli border (in a series of proposals to the United Nations Truce Supervisor, General Burns), the Gaza Raid provoked a determination to seek new armaments. After the February Israeli attack, incidents steadily increased and the clamour for positive action mounted. In August, 1955, after Israel had refused several Egyptian and U.N.T.S.O. proposals to reduce frontier tension, the Egyptian Government reached a fateful decision to organize para-military commando units, the *fedayin*, for raids into Israel. While the strength of these units, and the duration of their activity, was greatly exaggerated, it is the writer's personal opinion that this decision was not only immoral, but tactically unwise. That refugee anger against Israel had reached crisis-point, there is no doubt; and it has been held by many observers that the organization of the *fedayin* may have averted far worse consequences. The bloody nocturnal character of their activities, however, must surely stand as a regrettable stigma on Colonel Nasser's record.

The Czech Arms Deal

In April, 1955, Britain adhered to the Baghdad Pact, and thereby earned the complete opprobrium of Arab nationalists. In the same month, Colonel Nasser's role as a major statesman at the historic Afro-Asian Conference of Bandoeng reinforced Arab enthusiasm for his leadership. At Bandoeng, Chou En-lai offered Nasser Chinese arms. Nevertheless, throughout the summer and early autumn of 1955, he continued earlier efforts to secure new arms, without political conditions, and in quantity, from Britain and the United States. The Western Powers, however, were confronted by the very real dilemma, formalized in the Tripartite Declaration of 1950, of trying to maintain the Armistice *status quo* in Palestine by ensuring a rough balance of military power between Arabs and Israel. In addition, both Governments were less and less disposed to consider giving arms to an Egyptian Government that so resolutely and vociferously opposed their cold-war policies in the region.

In September, 1955, Egyptian-Israeli tension and arms competition came to a head. On September 21st, Israeli forces invaded and occupied the triangular area around El-Auja, on the Armistice line with Egypt, which had been formally registered as a demilitarized zone in the Armistice. On September 28th, Colonel Nasser announced that Egypt had contracted to buy considerable quantities of new weapons, including munitions factories, from Czechoslovakia. The extent of this Egyptian financial commitment, and the very fact of so significant a Soviet-bloc entrée into the Middle East, caused widespread concern in the West. Nasser publicly emphasized that the deal did not alter Egyptian neutralism; that Arab nationalism would not embrace Communism; and that he had taken up the Soviet-bloc offer, as a straightforward commercial transaction, only after protracted efforts to secure arms from Western sources. But in the West the decision seemed to open the gates of the Middle East—and therefore Africa—to Soviet penetration.

It was thereafter widely assumed in the West that Egypt's Czech deal had completely upset the balance of armed strength with Israel, and that Israel later—

and only later—sought to redress the balance by procuring new armaments from France. Early in November, 1955, however, Nasser told a *Life* magazine reporter that the Czech decision had been taken, not so much in terms of Israel's strength as it was then, as in terms of her strength when her existing secret arms arrangements with France were completed. He detailed the types and quantities of French weapons to be delivered to Israel. The next day, Israeli spokesman denied the existence of any arms deal with France at all. But in 1956, when French arms deliveries to Israel were revealed, it was notable that they matched very closely, in type and quantity, the details which Nasser had professed to know in 1955.

1956—a Year of Crisis

The conflict between Western traditional and current policy, and the vigorous new nationalism led by Nasser, rapidly worsened in 1956. In December, 1955, General Templer had arrived in Amman to urge Jordan to join the Baghdad Pact. There was widespread protest and disorder, and the effort had to be abandoned. The Jordanian army—the Arab Legion, commanded by Sir John Glubb—was used to repress the demonstrations and, in consequence, Glubb Pasha became the even greater focus of anti-British resentment. Again, there was a widespread tendency in the West to attribute this unrest solely to the machinations of Cairo. The elder, conservative political leaders in Jordan, Iraq and elsewhere—the "good" Arabs—reinforced this reaction in their discussions with Western diplomats and journalists.

It was also in December, 1955, that the United

States and Britain determined to try to counteract the Soviet bloc's new prestige in Egypt by agreeing to negotiate two major loans for the construction of the giant High Dam project at Aswan. One loan was to be a combined Anglo-American offer; a second would follow from the World Bank, whose experts advised that the plan for the dam was sound. Detailed talks with Egypt began, and were described quite frankly by authoritative Western commentators as an Anglo-American cold-war gambit, albeit with an increasingly disliked régime.

The month of March, 1956, brought a series of events throughout the Arab world that dramatically reflected the accelerated pace of nationalism. Both in Morocco and in Tunisia there were formalities and celebrations marking the independence of these former French territories. While there is no evidence of a deliberate policy decision of the kind, the loss of Morocco and Tunisia served to strengthen French determination to retain Algeria. It also increased French anger over Egypt's support to the Algerian nationalist rebellion. On the other hand, the fact that Morocco and Tunisia had won independence inevitably raised the morale of nationalism in general throughout the whole region.

In the Arab East, Egypt, Syria and Saudi Arabia formally concerted their policies of neutralism at a meeting in Cairo, thus increasing the direct challenge to the Western Baghdad Pact initiative. It was in Jordan, however, that the most dramatic and conse-quential event of March took place. After the "Templer Riots", there was no longer any serious question of Jordan entering the Baghdad Pact. But nationalists in the Kingdom, who had for two years tried to persuade the boy King Hussein to terminate Jordan's special

British connections, now increased their suasion. The young man, part-aristocrat in the old Hashemite desert tradition, part-British from Harrow, Sandhurst and the long period of tutelage of his country, could no longer ignore the nationalist argument that he himself and his Throne were involved in Britain's unpopularity. Between January and March, however, he hesitated between the urgings of the nationalists who had access to him and the counter-urgings of Glubb Pasha, British diplomats, and the elder circle of Jordanian politicians. Then, near the end of February, Hussein read in a British magazine that Glubb was really the "uncrowned king of Jordan". On March 1st, 1956, the distinguished British soldier, who had devoted most of his life to service of a Jordan now changed beyond his recognition, was summarily dismissed.

Glubb Pasha flew to London and advised Sir Anthony Eden that his dismissal was the work of Egypt, and of a mere handful of "extremists" in Jordan; but wisely counselled against any abrupt action. At the same moment, the Foreign Minister, Mr. Selwyn Lloyd, was touring the Middle East. He was dining with Nasser when the news of Glubb's dismissal was brought to the Egyptian Prime Minister at table. Nasser thereupon informed Mr. Lloyd, who at once concluded that the ouster of Glubb had been carefully timed by Nasser, in Cairo, to humiliate Britain through her Foreign Minister. As Jordan erupted in celebration, Mr. Lloyd flew to Bahrein, where he met more demonstrations of protest. He, his advisers in Bahrein, and Britain's elder-Arab friends again attributed these to timed orders from Cairo. It was by such events that a picture was steadily developed of an Arab world in turmoil solely by plan and order of an Egyptian megalomaniac; a world in which, without his sinister hand, France in the Arab West and Britain in the East would not be challenged as to their traditional interests, nor the three Western Powers as to their cold-war policies. It need hardly be stressed, today, that this picture greatly over-estimated Colonel Nasser's personal aims or abilities; increasingly obscured a tide of opinion in each country that had developed years before Arabs heard of Nasser; and precipitated outright conflict which Western statesmen regarded as with the Egyptian leader, but Arabs increasingly interpreted as attack upon themselves.

It was the unfortunate fate of 1956 to bring each of the three Western Powers to this conflict by at least partially separate routes: France via Algeria; Britain via the Baghdad Pact, the ouster of Glubb, and other challenges to her traditional position in the area; the United States via the overall issues of Arab neutralism (which Mr. Dulles held to be "immoral") and Soviet penetration.

The High Dam Crisis

In mid-July, the Egyptian régime decided to accept the Western offers for High Dam loans, and the Ambassador flew back to Washington with this decision, which he made public on reaching New York. The World Bank had reaffirmed its approval of the plans for the dam and its offer a few days before. On July 19th, when the Egyptian Ambassador met Mr. Dulles to discuss the decision, a British Foreign Office spokesman repeated Britain's readiness. That afternoon, however, as the Egyptian envoy left Mr. Dulles, the U.S. State Department issued to the press a brief prepared announcement withdrawing the loan offer because, it was alleged, Egyptian economic conditions had deteriorated. The British Government, supposedly not advised beforehand, followed suit, as did the World Bank. Britain's real part remains in doubt.

Secretary Dulles' calculations for this almost unprecedentedly terse and derogatory announcement are still not fully known. It is generally held that, apart from Congressional opposition to the loan, he sought to administer a sharp and public rebuke to Arab neutralism. Authoritative press comment referred to Nasser's "playing off East against West" over the dam loans, for the Soviet Union had earlier let it be known that she would enter the loan contest. The original Western offers were, of course, designed to compete in precisely this manner.

If the U.S. Secretary's motives are not yet documented, nor are his expectations of the results. It was not, however, difficult to estimate what these would be. They could only encompass Nasser's downfall, later if not sooner, or precisely the kind of angry riposte of which it was already known that he was capable. It is historically important to note that, of the two possibilities, Arabs themselves expected only his downfall, in the resigned belief that no leader could survive direct pressure from a Western Power. In every major Arab capital, as in Cairo, there was open speculation as to Nasser's successor.

The Canal Company Nationalization

On July 21st, President Nasser, in evident anger, told a mass audience that Egypt would build the High

Dam regardless (Moscow had let it be known that a Russian loan would not be forthcoming). Of the United States he spoke in a Kuranic allusion that shocked Americans. Translated without regard to semantic differences between Western tongues and the intrinsic exaggeration of Arabic, the reference reached Americans as: "Let them choke to death in their fury." The Kuranic proverb, in fact, conveyed to Arab listeners little more than the force of an Americanism like; "They can go jump in the lake: we will do what we set out to do." (The exact phrase was *falya-moutu bighayzihim*.) The incident was symptomatic of a wider and continuing problem of semantics in the Western-Arab conflict. On this occasion, it heralded momentous crisis.

On July 26th, as Sir Anthony Eden and Mr. Selwyn Lloyd were dining with Nuri es-Said in London, news of Nasser's announcement was brought to them. The Suez Canal Company was to be nationalized; shareholders would be compensated; foreign currency revenues from Canal tolls would be used to help build the High Dam.

For most Arabs, there was sheer astonishment and incredulity. A new and young nationalist leader (Nasser was only thirty-eight), whose downfall had seemed so certain, had seized the initiative and struck back at a major Western rebuff through a Company long synonymous with Western hegemony. Arabs were not accustomed to this kind of courage, impassioned determination, and "staying power". In a society highly susceptible to vigorous leadership, this new act completed a picture of Nasser that already included cardinal and—again—traditionally rare virtues of frugal personal living, incorruptibility, simple and direct speech, and a capacity to echo popular feelings. Even among those educated Arabs—and they were many—who regarded Nasser's abrupt and angry action as intemperance verging on irresponsibility, there was an underlying admiration and a new sense of dignity.

The Western reaction was the very opposite. The Suez Canal was a vital international waterway; the Company that had operated it for almost a century was solemnly contracted to and with Egypt. The sudden, unilateral seizure, following on many earlier events so grimly interpreted in the West, was compared by Eden with Hitler and a potential "Munich". In France, historic sentiment about French construction of the Canal, anger over French financial and administrative interest in the Company, and continuing outrage over Cairo's support of the Algerian nationalists, impelled M. Mollet to the conviction that President Nasser must be overthrown. In Britain Sir Anthony Eden, a trained Arabist in the old aristocratic tradition, brought up to think of the Canal as "almost a part of England", and with trenchant personal memories of Munich, reached the same conclusion. In Washington, Mr. Dulles was no less shocked by what he deemed an irresponsible assault on international morality and law. Describing President Nasser's anger over the withdrawal of the High Dam loan offer as "fancied grievances", the U.S. Secretary, however, from the very outset wisely opposed the use of force. As Anglo-French forces were despatched to the eastern Mediterranean, and combined staff planning for an expedition began, Mr. Dulles bent every effort to dissuade his trans-Atlantic colleagues from such measures.

Enough is already known of the official attitudes

involved in the Suez crisis to justify the observation that its origins lay far earlier than July 19th (the U.S. Aswan loan withdrawal) or July 26th (President Nasser's nationalization speech). The underlying Western-Arab conflict was already in full course, as we have seen. It may be said, however, that if Mr. Dulles gravely underestimated President Nasser, and the extent to which he was the enactor, the product, and the spokesman of a generation, President Nasser also grossly underestimated Western views. He did not appreciate the depth of indignation and alarm engendered in the West by his brand of leadership and his propaganda. The policies he initiated at the beginning of 1955 challenged many traditional, deeply-rooted Western assumptions and attitudes—challenged them far more gravely than he and his colleagues, from their vantage-point, could perceive. If this mutual lack of contact was evident before July, 1956, it was sharply underlined by the fact and the manner of Nasser's response to Mr. Dulles. The idea of nationalizing the Suez Canal Company was in no way novel: such a demand had been made by Egyptians even before World War I, before Nasser was born. It was perhaps inevitable that Egyptians should place an altogether different value on the contractual relationship by which the Company operated the Canal. A wiser, more sober Egyptian leader, however, would have reflected that every facet of this waterway touched Anglo-French susceptibilities to the very quick; and that abrogation of the contract with the Company, in the political atmosphere already prevailing, would provoke great alarm and afford Eden a pretext for attack.

This search for a pretext was indeed evident in the

official Anglo-French arguments, which, over three months of negotiations were, to say the least, specious. The basic legal guarantee of free access to the Canal lay in the 1888 Convention, to which Egypt was a signatory. The additional guarantee, to Britain, had lain in the concrete fact of her military occupation of Egypt (until 1936) and of the Suez Canal Zone (until 1956). On the day when, in May, 1956, the last British soldier left the Zone, free access to the Canal rested entirely on the 1888 Convention, Egypt's respect for it (under whatever Government), and the ability of the maritime powers to enforce such respect through the International Court and the U.N. Charter.

The nationalization of the Company did not affect this position. It did, however, raise legitimate questions for world users of the waterway: (1) Would Egypt reaffirm respect for the 1888 Convention? (2) Would she maintain equitable and non-discriminatory tolls? (3) Would she operate and maintain the Canal in consonance with its established importance to world maritime trade? (4) Would she develop it to keep pace with steadily increasing traffic? Between July 27th and October 24th, 1956, the Egyptian Government did in fact give a satisfactory answer to each of these legitimate concerns—including President Nasser's early offer to conclude a new treaty of free navigation and deposit it with the United Nations. October 29th, the date of the Sinai attack that was followed by Anglo-French military assault on Egypt, was also the date when the principal parties to the dispute were due to meet at Geneva under U.N. auspices. On that date, there was ample ground for the conviction that the legitimate concerns of world users could be met by peaceful negotiation with Egypt.

The Effects of Sinai and Suez

The brief war did not accomplish its objectives. It destroyed, not the Nasser Government, but an era of Anglo-French relations with the Arab world. The Israeli attack, so clearly implicated in the Anglo-French military plans, confirmed in the Arab mind the forty-year old fear of Zionism and the Jewish State as "an aggressive, expansionist force" using and used by imperial powers.

To the Soviet Union, for its part in halting the triple attack, there accrued an access of prestige among Arabs which—it is surely safe to say—Soviet leaders could not have secured in years of effort on their own. To the United States, for a very brief period afterwards, there accrued almost equal gratitude: a momentous fund of Arab expectations, not only because of the U.S. condemnation of Anglo-French use of force, but because an American President had also opposed a Zionist action in the midst of an election campaign.

Neither the triple attack, Egypt's supposed defeat in Sinai, nor the fact that the war was halted by foreign initiative weakened President Nasser in his role of leader of Arab nationalism. The evident expectation of Anglo-French authorities that he would resign or be overthrown proved incorrect: he announced his intention of remaining in Cairo, issued rifles to civilians, and moved openly through crowded streets. His Government did not admit a military defeat in Sinai, but the facts were soon known widely in the Arab world. That these did not seriously weaken Egyptian prestige was less surprising than many Western observers held it to be. There was not, in fact, an Egyptian

defeat until the Egyptians were ordered to withdraw
from the desert in face of the Anglo-French threat to
the Canal Zone in the rear. It was no paradox whatever
that the nationalist movement emerged from the whole
crisis with a sense of moral victory; and that Nasser
emerged, if anything, with his stature in some ways
enhanced (save, perhaps, among Palestine Arab refugees
who had hoped for a final Palestine "solution").

The crisis and war might indeed be described as
another Palestine. It was an episode stimulating each
basic aspiration: complete independence from all
external influence; urgent social reform; closer Arab
unity; and region-wide neutralism. In this aftermath,
the vital difference was that only one Western Power
now remained in an effective position to come to terms
with Young Arabism. The entire burden of imagina-
tive diplomacy to counter the new Soviet prestige, and
rebuild Western-Arab relations on a new basis, rested
on the United States.

The Eisenhower Doctrine

It was in this vacuum, not of "influence" but of Arab
expectations, that the United States, in January, 1957,
formulated the "Eisenhower Doctrine". While it
continued to elude clear definition, American policy—
more or less proclaimed to be pursuing this Doctrine
—rapidly evolved in two forms. There developed, on
the one hand, what might be described as a kind of
"subscription list" against international Communism;
for those Arab Governments which signed it, U.S.
economic and military aid was forthcoming. This arm
of post-Suez American policy developed in tune with
repeated statements that there was, in fact, a "vacuum

of influence" in the Middle East, with the implication that either America or Russia would fill it. This thesis was, of course, deemed both insulting and inimical by nationalists who, in the Arab world as elsewhere, derived their very aspirations from the conviction that they could and should replace all foreign influence themselves. This entire American thesis, combined with the subscription-list character of the new U.S. economic and military aid programme, quickly persuaded Arab nationalists that the Eisenhower Doctrine was an instrument of cold-war pressure.

The other facet of U.S. policy in the Middle East post-Suez was a concerted effort to achieve what soon became widely described as "isolating Nasser". The United States reaffirmed support for the Baghdad Pact. The attitude of the Iraqi Government of Nuri es-Said towards the Egyptian Government and its supporters was clear. The "isolation" policy was also implemented with especial emphasis on Saudi Arabia, Lebanon and Jordan. Early in 1957 King Saud, Lebanon's President Chamoun, and Iraq's Crown Prince Abdul-Ilah were received in Washington. The initiative in Jordan was necessarily of a different character, as will be seen in a moment. The general objective was to support those Arab régimes willing to subscribe to the Doctrine, in the hope that a major counter-force to "Nasserism" could be created. For reasons indicated earlier, such régimes were—almost by definition—led by the older, ultra-conservative political order of monarchs, autocrats and wealthy oligarchies (the "good Arabs"), who were bound to oppose the impulses towards reform and unity expounded by the movement led by Nasser. As such, these régimes were unpopular. In Western commentary, however, they became known as "pro-Western" and, by a significant process of projecting idealized images from such a label, were deemed popular. It thus came about that the United States Government inherited from Britain virtually the whole body of traditional relationships and interpretations whose obsolescence had so contributed to the crises of 1956.

Finally, American policy outside Egypt was combined with a policy of attrition within Egypt, designed, presumably, to weaken the Nasser Government at home. Egyptian dollar assets remained frozen (together with franc and sterling assets). U.S. economic and technical aid to Egypt remained suspended. In January, 1957, a serious crisis of supplies arose. Egyptian stocks of wheat were adequate for no more than two weeks, and of oil for four days. Penicillin and other vital medical supplies were exhausted. The Egyptian Government asked Washington for emergency assistance, which was refused; and then for the release of such Egyptian dollar assets held in the United States as would enable the purchase of these emergency supplies. This was also refused. Egypt then approached Russia and secured immediate, unconditional assistance. By the end of February Egyptians concluded, from the very colour of their flour (very inferior, but at least extant), that Russia had again proved a "friend in need". In subsequent months, and until early 1958, the continued freezing of Egyptian dollar as well as sterling and franc assets progressively forced a complete reversal of the country's foreign trade structure, from 75 per cent. with the West before Suez to 75 per cent. with the Sino-Soviet bloc.

Throughout this process, Western statesmen frequently commented adversely on the trend, although it was not clear in what manner Western policy was helping to correct it.

The Jordan Crisis

Apart from the general tide of ideas in the Arab world, which was not—it would seem—evident to United States policy-planners, official expression of these ideas in early 1957 came from Egypt, Syria and Jordan. American relations with the Syrian Government deteriorated rapidly within weeks of the Sinai-Suez War, as the result of a major, though wholly incorrect, wave of apprehension outside Syria that the chief of the Deuxième Bureau, Lieut.-Colonel Abdul Hamid Serraj, was a Communist, and intended to subvert Syria into a Soviet satellite. The net result was that all possible opportunity for better relations between the U.S. and Syrian Arab nationalists was rapidly lost.

In pursuit of the American objectives already outlined, there thus remained the Kingdom of Jordan. Just before the Sinai-Suez War, the country's first genuine elections had returned a majority in parliament expressing all the basic themes of Young Arabism. The new Prime Minister, Suleiman Nabulsi, immediately announced and won parliamentary approval of several policies implementing these ideas. They included recognition of the Soviet Union and China, previously forbidden; non-alignment in the cold war; abrogation of the Anglo-Jordanian Treaty giving Britain military bases in the country; replacement of British subsidies by Egyptian, Syrian and Saudi

Arabian subventions; and negotiations for federal union with Syria (which, since the Syrian Government desired federal union with Egypt, would include the latter).

Premier Nabulsi emphasized that Jordan would not replace British influence with that of any other foreign country. He expressed the hope that the United States would give Jordan unconditional aid; and announced that his Government would seek new armaments, which he would prefer to buy from the West. Whatever fears might be entertained about the opening of diplomatic relations between Moscow and Peking and yet another Arab State, the Nabulsi Cabinet could not be judged Communist or pro-Communist, either in its composition or policies.

It was not surprising, however, that the young King Hussein was unhappy about the prospect of Jordan's union with republican Syria and, very probably, with republican Egypt. Given his background and upbringing, it was natural that he should fear for his Throne. He quite sincerely identified it with the destiny of the people of Jordan. The elder political leaders of the *ancien régime* no less naturally encouraged him in these views. But Hussein's very popularity among his people, since the departure of Glubb Pasha, rested on the fact that he had shown his apparent support for their aspirations. He had allowed the first free elections; had accepted the resultant Cabinet; had apparently approved its statement of policy, including union with Syria and abrogation of the special British connexion. In short the boy-King had unleashed, and in the eyes of the people had become identified with, popular goals whose ultimate effects on his own position he began to fear more and more.

It was from this unenviable standpoint that Hussein and his elder advisors perceived in the Eisenhower Doctrine a possible solution. The King could not oppose the abrogation of the treaty with Britain and the end of British subsidies. Unless some alternative source of financial support for Jordan's artificial economy could be found, the country must inevitably be brought closer and closer to union with the two republics offering to replace the British subsidies. In January, 1957, the U.S. Government refused Prime Minister Nabulsi's request for unconditional aid. But it was separately intimated to the Palace that U.S. aid could be given a Jordan eschewing relations with Moscow and Peking and pronouncedly staying outside the Egyptian-Syrian neutralist orbit. It was further explained that express endorsement of the Eisenhower Doctrine—rapidly becoming so unpopular among Arab nationalists—would not be necessary, provided the U.S. Congress had clear evidence of strong anti-Communist control of Jordan.

In subsequent weeks, King Hussein's relations with his Cabinet increasingly deteriorated—not least as a result of his making public a significant letter to the Prime Minister warning against "international Communism", a letter released without the prior and constitutionally required approval of the Jordanian Cabinet. This growing Palace-Cabinet conflict was still very largely secret, however. King Hussein remained popular, together with his Cabinet. The appearance of common aims of nationalism between King and Cabinet was reinforced by the celebrations over the end of the Anglo-Jordanian Treaty. Thus, by March, 1957, official Jordanian politics were in a peculiar *impasse*. The King had his private assurances of U.S. financial support to keep Jordan independent, but his popular Cabinet was preparing to recognize Moscow and Peking and to proceed towards union with Syria. The King could not publicly oppose this policy; nor could the Cabinet, if it wished, depose the popular young monarch.

In April, 1957, this Palace-Cabinet conflict came to a head, when King Hussein announced "plots" against him and his Throne and dismissed the Nabulsi Government. Supported by *ancien régime* politicians, he accused Nabulsi, the various nationalist parties, and Egypt and Syria of, variously, bringing Communism, the Eisenhower Doctrine, Egyptian control, and even Israeli danger, to Jordan. The young King was able to count on the loyalty of Bedouin units in the army, and as these spread out over the country nationalists were arrested, driven underground, or compelled to go into exile. The United States rushed the Sixth Fleet to the eastern Mediterranean and warned that paratroops might be used to preserve "the independence and integrity of Jordan". By the end of April, with the little kingdom under tight martial law, the "Jordan Crisis" was over. King Hussein received an immediate grant of $10 million from Washington.

The King's version of the "plots" has been largely accepted in orthodox Western accounts. Suffice it to say here that closer enquiry indicates that the King himself may have staged the plots in order to impugn the Nabulsi Cabinet on the one charge that might— but did not—earn public sympathy. It was significant, though not noted in the West, that Cairo Radio did not attack the King throughout the month of crisis. This silence alone makes the "plots" doubtful.

Thereafter, Jordan remained under martial law for nearly two years. In the West, as Egyptian and Syrian propaganda against him and the United States did then vociferously begin, Hussein's action was judged to be that of a courageous young monarch saving his country from "pro-Communist domination". The victory for "pro-Western and anti-Nasser forces" so widely hailed in the West, however, confirmed in the minds of Arab nationalists throughout the region that the United States had adopted the gunboat diplomacy of Britain. Seen in the broad context of the chasm of misunderstanding we are here tracing, it was surely symptomatic that the only Western Power then able to correct Arab suspicions of the West had in fact assisted in the overthrow of the first popular, fairly elected Cabinet in Jordan's history.

The Lebanese Civil War

The second major repercussion of U.S. policies pursued in the general name of the Eisenhower Doctrine occurred in Lebanon. The Republic (pop. 1,450,000) is approximately half-Christian and half-Moslem, the former being for the most part of the Maronite Church (autonomous, but in communion with the Roman Catholic Church). Lebanese Christians have been there since Christianity itself. They therefore feel themselves rooted in the Middle East, but, since the first massacre of Christians in 1860, look to the West both culturally and for protection. Lebanese Moslems, on the other hand, no less naturally feel close bonds of culture and political sentiment with their Arab neighbours.

In 1943, when Lebanon was liberated from Vichy-French control and independence appeared to be in sight, Christian and Moslem leaders concluded a "gentlemen's agreement", known as the Pact of 1943. It provided, in essence, for an independent Republic whose denominations would agree to compromise between their respective sensibilities and live in harmony. The President of Lebanon should be Christian, and the Prime Minister Moslem. A similar distribution became the tradition for the whole structure of political and administrative life, with Christians retaining a slight advantage. Most importantly, it was mutually accepted that Lebanon was to be an Arab country. Christians would not demand alliances with any Western Power, in return for which Moslems would agree to Lebanon's sovereign detachment from her Arab neighbours.

The 1956 Sinai-Suez War caused acute tension in the Republic. Angry Moslem (and some Christian) nationalists demanded, at the least, the severance of diplomatic relations with Britain and France. The prevailing Christian leadership vehemently opposed such steps. The brevity of the attack on Egypt, combined with mutual restraint and sternly impartial public security measures, happily averted internal catastrophe. A new Cabinet was formed amid general relief that, as the Lebanese press proclaimed, "The Pact of '43 Stands Firm!" But the President, M. Camille Chamoun, supported by wealthy conservatives and a considerable proportion of Christians, remained hostile to Nasser's leadership of an increasingly dynamic and widespread Arab nationalism. It was feared that this movement's combined attractions might arouse Lebanese Moslems towards closer unity with their neighbours, and even affect the prevailing social and economic order within Lebanon.

With the formulation of U.S. post-Suez policy, a grave decision was taken. In Washington it was felt that the leadership of M. Chamoun and the new Lebanese Foreign Minister, Dr. Charles Malik (a pronounced friend of America), provided excellent opportunities for Lebanon to become a focal point of the Eisenhower Doctrine. Accordingly, an immediate effort was made to secure public endorsement of the Doctrine by the new Lebanese Government. The predilections of President Chamoun and Dr. Malik, the impact on Lebanese Christian opinion of the then fictitious alarum over Communism in neighbouring Syria, and the prospect of lavish economic and military aid contained in the Doctrine together produced the desired result.

United States aid began flowing to Lebanon, and U.S. warships paid courtesy visits to Beirut. In the spring of 1957 a general election was held and, as a result of unmistakable manipulation, a "pro-Western" majority was returned. Both before and after this election, however, tension steadily increased as the Opposition denounced the Government's adherence to the Doctrine as a violation of Lebanon's traditionally agreed neutrality. It was, again, unfortunate that this opposition was widely represented in the West as "pro-Communist" or artificially produced by Egyptian-Syrian subversion. It was seldom adequately appreciated that many very prominent Christians joined in opposing the Doctrine—including Lebanon's first President, who had proclaimed the "Pact of 1943", and the Patriarch of the Christian Maronite Church. (It cannot be seriously denied that the 1943 Pact had been gravely compromised, for it was cardinal in the Pact, and in the tradition it laid down, that Lebanese foreign policy must never cause her neighbours to regard the Republic as a base of Great Power pressure.)

In the winter of 1957-58 there were mounting reports of serious corruption and large-scale arms smuggling, including, most ominously, the apparent securing of arms by a long-outlawed neo-fascist party. In the spring of 1958, the point of crisis was reached when President Chamoun made it known that he wished to take a second term of office. Since this was unconstitutional, his supporters proposed to amend the Constitution. In the Opposition, the announcement was instantly interpreted as a further effort to perpetuate Doctrinal policy and the existing régime. In the midst of angry protest, an anti-Doctrine (Christian) editor was murdered, and breaking-point was reached. A general protest strike quickly erupted into civil war. It was not sectarian war: but as the conflict gathered pace the clear danger could be seen.

Syria and Egypt: The Union

Meanwhile, in Syria the Sinai-Suez War had accelerated nationalist demand for social reform, new arms, and closer unity with Egypt. In 1957 discussions began with Egypt, with emphasis on prior functional unity in such spheres as customs and tariffs, educational syllabuses, visas, and economic co-ordination. In respect of foreign aid, an opportunity for U.S. initiative appeared immediately after Suez, but quickly vanished. Syria had long been the most suspicious of all

Arab countries *vis-à-vis* the Western Powers. Nevertheless, the anxiety of the new Ba'athist-centred Cabinet to develop the Syrian economy brought about an approach to the World Bank for aid. The event was of the utmost significance, in that no previous Syrian Government had ever accepted official aid from any foreign source. The World Bank's terms for loans, however, proved too conditional. The opportunity for cautious and unconditional American aid might have remained, but the unfolding character of the Eisenhower Doctrine turned the Syrians away. It was in this manner that the Cabinet, in 1957, approached the Soviet bloc for unconditional aid, and yet another U.S. potential opportunity was lost.

As elsewhere in the world, Arab Communists—perhaps especially in Syria until 1958—had long sought opportunities for political gains through tactical alliances with non-Communist elements. In Syria's new approaches to Moscow for unconditional aid, and in Russia's prestige after Suez, Communists on the one hand and a coterie of conservative politicians of the old school on the other began to form such an alliance. In particular, Khaled el-Azm, one of the wealthiest magnates in the eastern Arab world, saw in the growing Soviet prestige his long-awaited and hitherto frustrated chance to achieve the Presidency of the Syrian Republic. He was Defence Minister in the Cabinet when, in August 1957, he signed a major Syro-Soviet aid agreement in Moscow. On his return to Damascus, he replaced the Army Chief of Staff by an officer more amenable to his, and to Communist, direction. By the end of 1957, it was clear to Ba'athists and non-Communist officers in the Army that el-Azm intended to use Soviet prestige to try to win the forthcoming 1958 parliamentary elections.

Syria had long been the focus and the prime source of the impulse towards closer Arab unity: Ba'athists in particular believed that the divisions in the Arab world were so entrenched, and so often fostered by foreign Powers, that they could be removed only by seizing "historic moments" of opportunity. Now such a moment—and a grave danger—seemed to have arrived. In January, 1958, Ba'ath leaders and nationalist officers flew to Cairo, explained the Communist-el-Azm danger to Nasser, and asked him to agree to immediate and total union of the two countries as the only certain and popular solution.

The proposal was quite new to Nasser. He had no plan of organic union with other states. In his mind Arab unity, at the current stage of what was a continuous revolution, meant above all "solidarity"—unity of key policies like neutralism and the kind of political, social and economic reform that would deny the Great Powers their traditional *ancien régime* support in the Arab world. Union with Syria—federal union—was being discussed, but even this looser association was to be achieved slowly and with careful planning. In short, and although this was not perceived in the West, the Egyptian President was a conservative, in the movement he led, as regards this vital goal of unity. But the danger posed by the Syrians was familiar to him and his colleagues—as also the danger that a drift towards Communism there might invite intervention by Nuri and the Western Powers.

The discussions in Cairo were therefore trenchant. Nasser and his colleagues began by urging the Syrians to achieve a genuine revolution and, in this way, to "set their house in order". The Syrians remained adamant about the danger. Nasser then laid down drastic conditions under which, and only under which Egypt would take on the responsibility and prestige-commitment of so drastic an union. It was the Egyptian hope that these conditions might act as a brake on Syrian thinking. But within two weeks the Syrian delegation had returned with all conditions—notably the dissolution of all political parties, including the Ba'ath Party—fully accepted, and with the blessing of the ailing Syrian President, Shukri el-Kuwaitly, a veteran exponent of Arab unity.

On February 4th, 1958, the United Arab Republic was proclaimed—the first organic union of two Arab countries in modern history. The news electrified the Arab world, being the first concrete expression of a vision implicit in the very word for nationalism—*qaumiyya*, or "peoplehood", the concept of one people, one nation. The crowds that greeted the event in Egypt and Syria were the largest in recorded history. But the popular symbol and figurehead of this dramatic occasion retained his doubts about the haste and lack of planning of the union. On February 5th, Nasser told the Egyptian National Assembly that the decision should involve caution as well as rejoicing. "Perhaps our uncurbed yearnings will prove to be the greatest danger we have to face," he said. "They have been released with the impetus of a long confinement, like a flood. . . . One of our primary duties is, through wisdom, to dam our aspirations. . . . This flow must be regulated, otherwise it may overwhelm us."

This significant statement was virtually unnoticed

in the West, where the union was generally interpreted
as an *Anschluss* by Nasser in Syria. (It might also be
added that, in the jubilation of the moment, it was little
heeded in the Arab world—partly because it was somewhat buried in Nasser's typically long and otherwise
polemical speech.) Western attention was focused on
the impact of the union elsewhere in the region. Those
régimes controlled by that older political order defined
earlier in this book as the West's "good Arabs" were
acutely apprehensive about the intoxicating effect of
the union. They promptly confirmed to Western
envoys and reporters the instinctive Western interpretation of an *Anschluss*. With evident U.S. and
British approval, Premier Nuri es-Said and King
Hussein then formed a rival Hashemite Federation
between the dynastically related monarchies of Iraq
and Jordan.

Change in Saudi Arabia

In the course of this new political crisis in the Arab
world, the politics of Saudi Arabia intruded. Despite
the absence of many of the most rudimentary institutions of modern statehood and society in his oil-
wealthy kingdom, King Saud was facing rising discontent in the towns and settled villages. This agitation
was both economic and social, and political; and it was
no accident that the symbolic leadership of Nasser
exerted no less attraction in the confines of the Arabian
Peninsula than outside it. King Saud's tentative involvement, in 1957, in the Eisenhower Doctrine was
not popular; nor was his later overt support for King
Hussein in the 1957 Jordan Crisis. Dissatisfaction was
not limited to the small but growing number of

educated and semi-educated people. The King's brother, Crown Prince Feisal, was widely travelled, somewhat more acquainted with modern Western precepts of society, and more sympathetic to the goals of the dominant Arab Nationalist movement.

In the course of Egyptian-Syrian celebrations of union, the new U.A.R. Government announced that a Saudi Arabian plot to prevent the union and assassinate President Nasser had been discovered. The charge was generally dismissed in the West as a fabrication designed to divert public unrest from an unpopular "annexation" of Syria. In later months, careful investigation by a small number of Western correspondents revealed that there had, in fact, been a Saudi plot (among other evidence was the resignation of the King's uncle from the Saudi Royal Commission established to examine the charge, and the fact that it never revealed its findings). In April, 1958, it was announced in Riyadh, the Saudi capital, that Crown Prince Feisal would assume most of the powers of government previously held by the King. While Saudi foreign policy made no abrupt *volte-face* thereafter, there was a pronounced reconciliation with Cairo and Damascus.

In subsequent months it became clear that the Crown Prince was determined to begin modernizing the kingdom's archaic institutions, and to attempt such judicious wider distribution of Saudi Arabian oil income as was possible while the Royal Family remained in power (a thousand princes and princesses had been consuming one-fifth of the annual income, £20 million, in personal allowances). Among concrete indications of this quiet, gradual internal revolution was the formation of the Kingdom's first proper Treasury, central banking institutions, and annual budget.

The Summer Crisis of 1958

In May, 1958, as already mentioned, the Lebanese civil war broke out. President Chamoun and Dr. Malik laid before the United Nations a charge of "massive intervention" in Lebanon, by the United Arab Republic, with the alleged purpose of subverting that country into the Egyptian-Syrian union. Both the United States and British Governments supported this charge, and in consequence the United Nations Observer Group in Lebanon (U.N.O.G.I.L.) was formed to determine whether infiltration of men and/or arms had taken place and, by its presence, to deter future possible infiltration. In a series of reports to the U.N. General Assembly from Lebanon, U.N.O.G.I.L. —eventually comprising more than 500 observer-officers from many nations—disproved the charge of massive intervention. There is little doubt that the Lebanese rebel Opposition did secure arms from abroad. But Opposition leaders maintained that these were commercial purchases, and justified the foreign purchase of weapons by citing the Government's issuance of state weapons—including arms delivered under U.S. aid—to unofficial groups supporting it. It was a peculiar and noted characteristic of the entire civil war that the official Lebanese Army, commanded by the neutral General Fuad Chehab, refused to obey Government orders to crush the rebels, which it could technically have done.

While the charge of "massive intervention" could

not be substantiated, virulent propaganda support by Cairo and Damascus against the Eisenhower Doctrine in Lebanon, and in favour of the rebel Opposition, was in no doubt. It was this, above all, that gave rise to the official Anglo-American thesis of "indirect aggression" by the U.A.R.—not only against Lebanon, but against Jordan, Iraq, Aden, and other Arab countries. The rise of this thesis epitomized the problem of Arab nationalism, and the lack of a comprehensive attitude to it in the West. Arabs were listening to Cairo and Damascus (in many instances asking radio dealers to tune their new set to "Voice of the Arabs" so that it might pick up the trusted station from the outset). They were so listening, literally to the number of millions, despite the fact that the Governments of their own countries possessed adequate radio stations; and in some cases on pain of prison from their Governments. The ideas and exhortations they heard from Cairo and Damascus manifestly corresponded to their own sentiments and grievances. Among the most powerful of these ideas was one that, in itself, challenged the whole thesis of indirect aggression— namely, the concept of an Arab nation, a "peoplehood" that *transcended* formal frontiers which, in many instances, were regarded as foreign (i.e., Western) creations.

Thus, for example, if Jordanians heard a Cairo radio commentator refer to King Hussein, after May, 1957, as a "traitor to the Arab cause", they again tuned into Cairo the following day because this appellation echoed their own attitudes towards a monarch who had dismissed a popular Cabinet and was ruling by martial law. They were not disposed to regard Cairo Radio as a "foreign" station in the sense in which the average Westerner would comprehend the word.

To return, however, to the Lebanese civil war, it remains to be noted that Opposition leaders repeatedly denied—as they had before the conflict—any desire to bring Lebanon into the United Arab Republic. This denial was strongly substantiated by the very character of the Opposition rebel force. It included the active belligerency of Christian and Druse groups whose leaders would unquestionably have opposed any such move. It was also significant that every former Foreign Minister of Lebanon since 1943 publicly opposed the charge laid against the U.A.R. by the Chamoun-Malik Government at the United Nations. It was unfortunate that vital indices of this kind were neglected in the West.

Revolution in Iraq

As the Lebanese civil war continued, tension rapidly mounted in the Middle East. American and British statesmen, convinced of the correctness of their interpretation of events, maintained the charge of indirect aggression and Egyptian imperialism. The popular impact of the Egyptian-Syrian union, the war in Lebanon, and evident Anglo-American support of President Chamoun, King Hussein and Nuri es-Said provoked increasing popular unrest. It was in these circumstances that Nuri es-Said, long in close accord with President Chamoun, came to the fateful decision. This was to enter Syria with a military force via Jordan, terminate the union with Egypt, and help to crush the Lebanese rebellion.

(This decision, of course, was not known publicly at

E

the time. It was revealed later, and has been assumed by Nuri's posthumous biographer, Lord Birdwood, M.V.O., who intimates official British knowledge of the plan.)

Opposition in Iraq to the existing triangle of power —Crown Prince Abdul-Ilah, Nuri es-Said, and the genuinely feudal tribal sheikhs—had remained unabated for many years. The Prime Minister's police measures and Army purgings, however, were so thorough that civilian opponents were powerless to act, and nationalist Army officers unable to organize. Nuri usually kept all doubtful units away from Baghdad. But in May, 1958, a number of Iraqi Army officers of brigadier level secretly agreed on a rough course of action: whosoever among them first found himself in or near Baghdad with the requisite ammunition and equipment would strike against the Government.

On the night of July 13th Brigadier-General Abdul Karim Kassem and his subordinate officer, Colonel Abdul Salaam Aref, got orders from Nuri. They were to proceed with their units to Jordan via Baghdad. On July 14th Colonel Aref led his columns into the city, with what momentous results a shocked and alarmed Western world learned a few hours later. When a detachment tried to arrest the boy-King Feisal and Crown Prince Abdul-Ilah, the latter opened fire. In the ensuing gun battle, most of the Iraqi Royal Family were killed. Nuri es-Said was killed while trying to escape, and his body defiled.

(The actual intentions of the revolutionary officers are not fully verified. It is reasonable to assume, however, that while Crown Prince Abdul-Ilah—the effective monarch for nearly two decades—might have been killed in any case, and would certainly have been brought to trial, the boy-King was the object of pity rather than hatred.)

For part of the day, conditions in Baghdad were reminiscent of Bastille Day in revolutionary France. The poor of the city, crazed with released anger and hideous vengeance, were in virtual control of the streets. It was in this period, before the Army suc-ceeded in restoring a modicum of order, that truly horrible things were done and many wholly innocent people disappeared for all time. The mass-psychological effect of the news of revolution was not unlike blowing off the cap of a long-simmering volcano, so grim were the conditions of many of Baghdad's poor, and so violent their opposition to the régime of Abdul Ilah and Nuri.

As an Iraqi Republic was proclaimed, and a new policy of neutralism announced, the revolutionary Deputy Premier, Colonel Aref, went to Damascus to greet President Nasser in the name of the revolution. In Western capitals there was instantaneous alarm over the first uncertain news of the revolt. President Eisen-hower called a meeting of the U.N. Security Council, but ordered U.S. forces to land in Lebanon before the U.N. had met. The British Government similarly ordered paratroops into Jordan. The exact motives behind these landings remain secret, but the evidence suggests an assumption that the Iraqi Revolution was planned in and executed on behalf of Cairo (U.S. intelligence agents added Moscow) and that an immediate "annexation" of Iraq by the United Arab Republic would be followed by the overthrow of King Hussein in Jordan and the Chamoun-Malik Govern-ment of Lebanon. In the hours that followed, an acute international crisis brought the world close to "the brink". In subsequent days the Government of Israel officially warned that any change in the *status quo* in Jordan would be deemed a threat over which Israel would "reserve full liberty of action".

The general crisis in the Middle East thereafter gradually abated. In Lebanon, where U.S. troops displayed exemplary restraint and discipline, but had no other apparent function, the civil war was brought to an end. M. Chamoun renounced his second-term Presidential intentions. Both sides agreed to the Presidency of the carefully neutral General Chehab, and under his impartial leadership a small Cabinet took power, representing both sides. American forces were withdrawn. The problem of the British troops in Jordan was rather more complicated, in view of Israel's warning and the likelihood of à revolt against King Hussein if and when British protection ended. The withdrawal of British troops was finally made possible by an all-Arab resolution in the U.N. General Assembly pledging non-interference between Arab states.

The New Iraq

As the Iraqi Army restored public order, two major decisions confronted the new Prime Minister, Abdul Karim Kassem, and his colleagues. There was on the one hand the vital question of the composition of the new government; and on the other, the new Republic's relations with the U.A.R. and President Nasser. These two problems were to prove interdependent, and Kassem's decisions on them led to grave consequences in the first year of the Republic.

So far as the first of them was concerned, the choice lay between forming an all-military government, or of bringing into the Cabinet leaders of the previously suppressed civilian parties. Brigadier Kassem was not an experienced politician; nor had it been possible, under the Nuri régime, to organize a cohesive officers' society with a council that might have undertaken the responsibilities of administration, at least *pro tem*. As a result, and under the advice of confidants whose political sympathies were not at first apparent, the new Prime Minister formed a largely civilian Cabinet.

At once, the issue of Iraq's Arab relations was thrust into the very nexus of authority in the new régime. By July of 1958, the tide of popular sentiment for Arab unity was running high. The great majority of Iraqis, convinced that the Nuri régime had kept Iraq isolated from their fellow-Arabs, regarded union with the U.A.R. as almost a *sine qua non* of the revolution. It was clear that either this expectation of early union with the U.A.R. must be met, or that refusal must be tempered by authoritative explanation of why it was undesirable.

To understand what followed, it may be useful to describe very briefly the various attitudes that produced conflict over this issue. We may begin with President Nasser. His earlier doubts about the haste of the Egyptian-Syrian union had increased. On July 22nd, at the precise moment when Iraqi expectations were highest, he pointedly referred in a major speech to the serious disadvantages of such haste, citing difficulties with the Syrian Budget that had been revealed only after the act of union because of inadequate prior study. He did not desire Iraq's organic union with the U.A.R.

in the immediate future, and secretly communicated this view to Premier Kassem. Their agreed policy was one of close functional unity only, for an undefined period. Kassem repeatedly stated that, while Iraq was "an integral part of the Arab nation", there would be a plebiscite at a later, undefined date, at which the people could choose their precise relations with other Arabs.

Nasser's conservatism on this issue earned him the private criticism of some of his highest supporters in and outside the U.A.R. In Iraq itself, his policy was in effect openly challenged by two forces. The first of these was the extremely popular symbolic leadership of the young Colonel Aref, the Deputy Premier, who had actually carried out the coup. Colonel Aref was passionate, impetuous, and not a little intemperate in his political pronouncements. A vigorous neutralist, he was openly anti-Communist as well as condemnatory of the Western Powers. Because Kassem was by nature reticent—even shy before the revolutionary crowds in his early months of power—the always vital role of orator of revolution passed by default to Aref, the "Hero of Baghdad". The young Colonel toured the Iraqi countryside demanding—indeed, almost promising—the union with the U.A.R. which he so passionately desired. At the same time, he made far-reaching promises on domestic policy that were as unsanctioned by the Cabinet as they were irresponsible (i.e. the abolition of all private debts contracted before July 14th).

The other overtly unionist force in Iraq was the Ba'ath Party—the Iraqi wing of the intra-Arab party whose Syrian leaders had pressed on Egypt union with their country. The union that Ba'ath sought was organic, not merely federative.

Against the demands of Colonel Aref and Ba'ath there stood two particular political forces released from suppression by the events of July 14th. The National Democratic Party, led by the veteran Iraqi socialist, Kamel Chaderchi, took the historical view that Iraq had never been a part of any wider Arab entity, and had a deservedly separate personality. Chaderchi and his fellow-Democrat leaders believed that a Western-style party-parliamentary democracy should now be created in the new Republic—and could be instituted immediately. Since party activity had been abolished in the United Arab Republic, the National Democrats were determined to resist the Aref-Ba'ath demand for a union which they feared would produce the same non-party system in Iraq. It was inconceivable to them that the result of a revolution against dictatorship (by Nuri) should be another form of dictatorship. There were, among Democrat leaders and members, intellectuals and professionals of Marxist thinking—notably Ibrahim Kubbah, the economist. This Marxist wing of the Democrats became increasingly powerful when, as we shall see in a moment, the party formed a virtual tactical alliance with Iraqi Communists.

For Arab Communists, the Iraqi Revolution was a supremely important development. The movement had gone through several major phases since World War II, none of which had proved successful. The early hope of making Egypt the centre had been frustrated by Nasser's long repression of Communist party action. The great access of Soviet prestige in the Middle East in general since 1955 was a distinct advantage. But any capitalization of this advance required some base within the Arab region in which local, Arab Communism could achieve strong popular standing and eventually take power. In Syria this had been frustrated by the union with Egypt. By every reckoning, therefore, Iraq—with its grim land tenure conditions, its high rate of urbanization, and its ready supply of oil wealth for striking development—was a supreme opportunity, to be exploited at once.

The Communist programme for revolutionary Iraq was carefully evolved, and was evident literally on July 15th, when the party was first in the field with wall-slogans, demonstration groups, and quantities of leaflets calling for "Arab Federation and Soviet Friendship". The reference to "Arab Federation" revealed a judicious decision to meet the popular demand for union, but to guide it into only the loosest form of union, if even that.

The party was no less determined than the National Democrats to prevent the kind of union with the U.A.R., under Nasser's anti-Communist and non-party leadership, that Aref and Ba'ath were promoting. It can thus be appreciated that, in two vital respects, Communist and Democrat aims were identical—no union, and full party-political freedom. The Communist Party intended gradually to develop its popular standing, and to infiltrate key official and mass-organizational posts, while publicly supporting the symbolic "above-party" leadership of Brigadier Kassem. Many Communist sympathizers who became active on July 14th were not even known to be such by their revolutionary colleagues, and did not at first reveal their sympathies. Accordingly, they secured critical posts, including those of Deputy Chief of the Baghdad Police, Director of Baghdad Radio, press censor, and President of the Revolutionary Court.

To remove all serious dangers to this carefully phased plan, however, required the effective elimination from influence of Colonel Aref, the Ba'ath Party, and such other key political leaders as might be sympathetic to Arab union and President Nasser. These last included leaders of the Istiqlal (Independence) Party, whose policy might conveniently be described as favourable to union but ready to follow the pace set by Nasser and Kassem. But, above all, it was decided that Deputy Premier Aref must go. His pro-union speeches were a danger; his popular standing and strong temperament might, the Communists and Democrats felt, come to challenge the more pliable Prime Minister Kassem. Quite apart from these considerations, there was widespread concern over Colonel Aref's irresponsible domestic promises.

It was thus that, in successive steps, the young Deputy Premier was removed from influence and eventually posted away to Bonn, and, when he returned to Baghdad in circumstances still not verified, was arrested for treason. The progressive demise from office and then from virtually all public activity of Ba'ath members and Istiqlal leaders quickly followed. There are some grounds for believing that the Communist Party then accelerated its original plan, possibly in an access of confidence. Hitherto noncommittal officials increasingly revealed their pro-Communist sympathies in their duties in press censorship, radio propaganda, and the notorious conduct of the Court. Communist-led militants in the

Popular Resistance forces, the "Peace Partisans", and the trade unions showed increasing assertiveness.

Above all, a further phase of the overall plan, probably again accelerated, was put into effect in December, 1958. It was evidently the intention gradually to develop propaganda against Nasser's leadership of the general Arab nationalist movement; increasingly to suggest that the U.A.R. President was a "Western puppet"; and steadily to promote in Syria a climate of opinion against the union with Egypt and in favour of "Syria's more natural destiny with Iraq". With Iraq consolidated as a strong Communist base and a rising "showcase" of Arab "people's democracy", with Syria detached from Egypt and increasingly linked with Iraq, an expanding Communist movement could be launched into the Fertile Crescent.

It was in December, 1958, that the public attack against Nasser began—through Iraqi State organs as well as the controlled press—with the significant suggestion that he was "Washington's new friend". Almost immediately, Syrian Communists began a propaganda campaign against their country's union with Egypt. It was in consequence of these developments that the U.A.R. President began his counter-attack, first against Arab Communism in general and Egypto-Syrian Communists in particular, and then against the régime of Premier Kassem in Iraq. Thereafter, in the first months of 1959, the conflict between Arab nationalism, as led by Nasser, and Communism—involving Kassem—steadily developed. In March, 1959, a trainload of Communist-led "Peace Partisans" was sent to Mosul in northern Iraq to demonstrate. When they clashed with nationalists in the streets of the city, the Mosul army garrison commander telephoned to the Prime Minister in Baghdad asking him to order the Partisans to return to Baghdad. There was no answer from the Premier. The Mosul commander then began a spontaneous and ill-planned revolt, which signally failed, because anti-Communist officers in other parts of Iraq were not organized and ready to join it.

Between March and September, 1959, Premier Kassem showed belated signs of awareness that the Communists were moving closer and closer to full control of Iraq. He refused to accede to a Communist and Marxist-Democrat demand for strong Communist representation in the Cabinet. On the first anniversary of the revolution, in July 1959, Kassem declared all party-political activity suspended until 1960. But by the end of September these brief signs of sagacity about the Communist danger had been overshadowed by an event that deeply shocked and angered the Arab Middle East. In September, after a public trial in which prosecution witnesses had suddenly burst out with retractions of testimony which they said had been given under torture, thirteen Iraqi officers, accused of complicity in the Mosul revolt, were executed. To non-Communist Arabs inside and outside Iraq, this was taken as decisive evidence that Premier Kassem was still acceding to Communist demands.

Thereafter, the strange Prime Minister's public stock steadily declined, and in October, amid open signs of public unrest inside Iraq, he was wounded in an assassination attempt. He emerged from hospital after a protracted period of closely guarded convalescence, and in January, 1960, declared a resumption of political activity by parties so licensed. But the nationalist, anti-Communist wing of Iraqi politics had by then been gravely demoralized and disorganized—many of its most distinguished leaders having gone into exile or been intimidated into silence. These included not only the Ba'athists who had sought union with the U.A.R. (irrespective of Nasser's own wishes), but moderate Arab nationalists as well. For example, the Dean of Law at Baghdad College, a greatly respected Iraqi who had experienced jail under the Nuri régime, escaped from the country and publicly expressed his anguish over the drift of events under Kassem.

The role of the Prime Minister himself in all these critical first months of the Iraqi Republic remains an enigma. There is considerable evidence that Kassem's direction of Iraqi affairs has been deeply affected by two problems arising from his own personality : a long-developing monomania and a profound persecution complex. Combined with political inexperience and naïveté, these weaknesses apparently made him highly susceptible to the shrewd advice of Communists and Communist-sympathisers who moved into key positions in the new Government immediately after the 1958 revolution. They were able to persuade him, not only that he could and should remain altogether "above party" (as he repeatedly declares), but that almost every non-Communist Iraqi leader and group were plotting his demise and should therefore be liquidated. Convinced in his own mind that he was destined to be Iraq's "sole leader"—a term without precedent in modern Arab nationalist language—Kassem has tried now and then to exhaust all party-political forces below him by encouraging or allowing open conflict between

them. But the initial advantage given to the Communists, in the first wave of repression of anti-Communist groups, has to date served them well.

On the evidence to hand, this seems to explain why
a revolution impelled by all the familiar aims and
inclinations of non-Communist Arab nationalism
should have deteriorated to such a point that there is a
grave danger of Iraq becoming the first Communist-
controlled country in the Arab world. Above all,
Kassem's susceptibility to Communist suasions alone
explains why he did not take the early opportunity to
meet Nasser and jointly declare a moderate policy of
co-operation. It is one of the ironic facts of 1958 that,
had he accepted Nasser's four successive letters
suggesting a meeting wherever and on whatever
conditions he, Kassem, should designate, the Iraqi
Premier could have secured public support from the
U.A.R. leader both for himself and for a policy of
caution about any moves towards union.

At time of writing, the outcome of these tragic and
sanguinary months in Iraq is beyond prediction. The
country is undergoing a total, all-pervading socio-
economic upheaval; it was bound to do so, given the
forces unleashed after so many years of genuine
feudalism. It may, however, be predicted that unless
Premier Kassem can take the fundamental ideological
decisions which his "above party" doctrine dangerously
ignores, the new Iraqi Republic stands little chance of
non-Communist stability under his rule.

Change in the Sudan

Meanwhile, elsewhere in the Arab world the general
pace of political and social revolution increased—to no

small extent because of the electrifying impact of the Iraqi Revolution. In November, 1958, General Ibrahim Abboud led an army *coup d'état* in the Sudan, overthrowing the civilian Government and suspending Constitution and parties because of "the state of degeneration, chaos and national instability . . . [of] successive partisan governments". General Abboud proclaimed a foreign policy of neutralism, recognition of Communist China, intra-Arab co-operation, and efforts to secure especially close relations with Ethiopia and the United Arab Republic. The new officer-Premier described "artificial strain" with the latter country as among the major reasons for the coup. There was no indication, however, that General Abboud intended any move closer than that of co-operation with Cairo—with obvious concern that the two countries should reach agreement on the future of the Nile Waters. (This was signed in late 1959.)

It was significant, and symptomatic of a wider tendency, that General Abboud asserted that the Sudan had "perhaps not been ready for Western democracy when the British left". In the Sudan, as elsewhere where officer régimes had taken control, there was considerable public welcome for a strong, incorruptible and non-partisan executive.

Revolution in Yemen?

In mid-1959, there was also evidence of major political stirrings in the ancient and truly mediaeval Kingdom of the Yemen (the south-west corner of the Arabian Peninsula). Although the 70-year old Imam of Yemen was far less enlightened than even King Saud of Saudi Arabia, his son, Crown Prince al-Badr, had acquired modernist Arab-nationalist ideas. While the ailing Imam was in Italy for medical treatment—with his retinue of wives, concubines and slaves—the Crown Prince began a major purge of Yemen's officialdom, and announced that he was "determined to raise up this nation".

Crown Prince Badr had been largely responsible for Yemen's federation with the United Arab Republic early in 1958. He is by no means a fully emancipated modernist, but is an admirer of President Nasser. His reforms include the formation of a Representative Council and of a central Treasury and Budget—all three of which were previously lacking. There was no suggestion that the Crown Prince intended to usurp his father's authority. The reforms were more probably in response to a tide of dissatisfaction which expressed itself with greater freedom during the Imam's absence, and may yet challenge the whole Royal order. Yemen's federation with the U.A.R., the impact of foreign radio broadcasts, and the arrival in 1957 of technicians from Soviet-bloc countries to implement aid programmes, had all helped to open this corner of Arabia to the modern world.

Other Arabian States

The repercussions of revolution in the more advanced Arab countries were also felt in the chain of petty states and sultanates that fringe the Arabian Peninsula east of Yemen and around into the Persian Gulf. Arab nationalism exists and is constantly growing in the Federation of Aden, contiguous to Yemen and under special treaty relations with Britain. A striking example of this trend could be seen in 1958, when the

British Government forcibly deposed the young Sultan of Lahej, the ruler of one of the twenty-four principalities in the then Aden Protectorate, and the nominal chief Sultan among them. Sultan Ali ibn Abdul Karim had been fired by Arab nationalism, and by Nasser's leadership. Impatient over the special bonds between Lahej and Britain, he increasingly became the centre of political intrigue against H.M. Governor of Aden Colony, and set about modernizing his tiny sultanate.

In 1958 the Sultan went to London for discussions with the British Government and, while he was en route home, was deposed by British decree and the military occupation of Lahej. Subsequently, and in an effort to meet the tide of nationalism, Britain secured the Federation of the Adeni States. Their future, however, remains an unsolved problem—complicated by Yemeni claims of sovereignty over part of the western area, and by Britain's wish to retain the actual Colony of Aden (port and air-base) for strategic purposes. As British strategic bases further north have disappeared, the importance of Aden has steadily increased.

A second example of the impact of modern nationalism in this Arabian fringe area is evident in Kuwait, the fabulously wealthy sheikhdom (oil income £100 millions per annum, population 200,000) on the Persian Gulf immediately south of Iraq. The Sheikh of Kuwait, also under treaty relations with Britain, has devoted very considerable sums to the complete transformation of his Sheikhdom in education, housing, and public health and services. Kuwait's rapid modernization, however, has not blunted the edge of nationalism among its inhabitants—especially among the 50 per cent. non-Kuwaiti Arab population of Egyptians, Palestinians, Syrians and others brought in to provide the skills lacking among Kuwaitis. There is considerable local unrest over the disparity between the average Kuwaiti's income and the general luxury of the sheikhly family—an unrest in a sense increased, rather than assuaged, by the Sheikh's massive public investments. Another source of friction lies in the general conduct, not of the Sheikh himself, but of many of his autocratic relatives. The Sheikh's investment of Kuwait's enormous capital surpluses in the City of London attracts increasing resentment, and is allied to a nationalist demand for closer unity with the rest of the Arab world.

The revolution in Iraq in July, 1958, presented an immediate danger to the Sheikh, who pointedly and publicly met President Nasser in Damascus and expressed his sympathy with Arab nationalism. Communist activity in Iraq has also been a source of considerable concern. In general, it may be predicted that a major change in Kuwait's governance and external relations is bound to come. The resultant effect in the City of London (when Kuwaiti capital is re-directed to Arab development), and fear over Kuwaiti oil, will present Britain with a serious dilemma. The same general problem concerns the rest of the Arabian fringe-principalities. Frequent suggestions that military force might be used present a familiar prospect whose conquences scarcely bear contemplation. A major revision of British policy in these territories is long overdue, and cannot indefinitely be postponed.

CHAPTER SEVEN

THE INTERNAL ARAB REVOLUTION

THE EMPHASIS OF the preceding chapters has been on external issues—the clash between Arab nationalism and the Great Powers, the search for Arab unity, the conflict with Israel. It has also been a theme of this survey, however, that these international crises had powerful currents of internal Arab socio-economic change; and that if these had been appreciated, much of the storm might have been avoided. A profound and continuous internal Arab revolution has been to a great extent concealed from world notice—partly because nationalist leaders themselves have constantly addressed their public utterances to the external issues and have most certainly been preoccupied by them; but partly, too, because ideas about Arab society in the West have continued to be based on images of Arabian Nights potentates and harems, of venal politicians indifferent to filth and poverty, and of "ignorant mobs".

The process of socio-economic change in the Arab world, and the problems it presents, involve virtually every aspect of human life, on a scale varying from the wholly medieval to the modern. In the Yemen, there still exist women with iron rings driven through their arms as punishment. In Egypt, even the traditional woman's veil is disappearing so rapidly that the change can be noticed from year to year. In Saudi Arabia, a thief's hand may still be cut off—but the stump may now be sterilized by a doctor. In very many Arab countries, however, legal systems are modern, and programmes of public health and medical welfare have advanced so strikingly that population increase is a critical problem.

Rapid advances in public education, health, communications and industry were made under the Mandate and other administrations during what has been earlier described as the thirty interim years from 1922 to 1952. But the measures taken were insufficient, especially in rural areas; the politico-economic philosophy of the régimes of the period was *laissez-faire*; corruption was widespread; and while the wealth of great landowners and magnates increased, the poverty of an ever-larger mass of Arabs was not alleviated. Against these conditions, and under the influence of modern Western ideas, nationalists of the new generation have approached their revolutions with a consciousness of social and economic need that should not be dismissed by an impatient West merely because Arab society has not yet been transformed.

In its internal goals, modern Arab nationalism is overwhelmingly secular, and socialist. In the Arab awakening of the nineteenth and twentieth centuries, while many individual thinkers turned to the ideal of a regenerated Islam as the basis of a new society, the institutions of Islam, such as they are, remained torpid relative to the influx of Western secular ideas. Nationalists like Bourguiba, Nasser, and the leaders of the radical (non-Communist) inter-Arab Ba'ath Party long ago decided that they could not find solutions to the internal problems of Arab society in the Kuran. It was significant that the constitution of the United Arab

Republic was drafted without a single reference to Islam: it is a completely secular document.

At the same time, it should not be thought that Islam, as a force in private Arab life—or even as an inchoate communal sentiment—is waning. Among illiterate peasant Arabs, the concept of membership of the *umma*, the Moslem community, may well be greater than any notion of membership of a "nation". This mass-role of Islam in nationalism needs urgent study. Its political consequences, however, are diminished not only by the secularism of nationalist leadership, but because the traditional sources of Islamic theology and social guidance have remained so relatively inert. An index might be seen in the fact that Nasser, having suppressed the Moslem Brotherhood in 1958 and launched a secular U.A.R. constitution, then appointed a new Rector to the ancient theological centre of Islam, El-Azhar University in Cairo. Rector Chaltout has since preached the emancipation of women, and has affirmed the complete compatibility of scientific thought with Islam. Arab nationalist leaders, many of them devout Moslems—many others no less devout Christians— recognize that an archaic Islam will retard the emancipation of the peasant. They may even regard a regenerated Islam as a source of strength and dynamism. But every major indication is that these contemporary leaders firmly believe in secular government and politics, and in a nationhood open to the three great Arab world religions (the Palestine conflict has not involved suppression of Judaism, vitally distinct from Zionism).

Turning to the socialist theme of modern Arab nationalism, it does not admit of easy description—

indeed, Western observers are often at pains to find any coherent socio-economic doctrine in the movement. The difficulty of evolving such a doctrine is not limited to the Arab part of the Afro-Asian world, but it is undoubtedly true that the obsession, for many decades, with external issues has prevented sustained, critical thought among Arab leaders. The problem is above all that where socialism, in an historically evolved, industrialized and economically stratified Western society, has certain clear objectives and implications, in Arab society these are either meaningless or impossible. The common denominator is, of course, the concept of the moral and necessary use of the state to direct and advance the human and material resources of a nation. But while Western socialism seeks a redistribution of existing wealth, Arab socialists are confronted by the problem that—save for the small "feudal" element—the only other "wealth" is that of the educated administrative, professional and commercial minority, *on whom the very functioning of the state and administration depends*. The number of wealth-producing utilities or industries to be "nationalized" is minute; they have to be founded in the first instance. While the emphasis is indeed on public investment for industry, the Arab socialist is confronted by the fact that, if he stifles private capitalism, he is stifling a vital locus of entrepreneurial skill and initiative which he cannot simply absorb into a civil service.

Again, socialism in agriculture may be a heady, emotive ideal, but in pragmatic terms it involves a clash with a deeply-rooted peasant proprietary instinct —an instinct reinforced by the fact that the peasant is illiterate and intensely suspicious of "government".

A simple way of expressing this problem might be to illustrate it by the case of the man who shares the produce of a single fig-tree with five brothers; who has difficulty in eking out a marginal existence for his family on a primitively tilled strip of land; and whose entire experience of authority connotes taxes, exorbitant rents, and usurious money-lenders supported by the police. Such a man will not simply hail an invitation to join a co-operative society.

In short, scepticism about the broad emotive professions of a "socialist and co-operative society" in Arab nationalism needs to be modified by awareness that no neat Western blueprint can solve Arab socio-economic problems. It is the spirit, not the practice, of Western socialism that the modern nationalist (or intellectual economist) has imbibed, and genuinely wishes to advance. He can do this only by experiment and ingenuity; he cannot *imitate*.

He begins with a great emphasis on public education, one of the most immediate and enthusiastic new steps after full independence. A mere glimpse of this may be seen in the fact that school attendance in Morocco soared from 287,000 in 1955 to over 625,000 by 1958. In Egypt, the Wafdist leadership of the thirty-year transition period described in an earlier chapter made tremendous strides in this field. One result was that by 1946 Egypt was producing eleven times more university graduates in proportion to population than was Britain. Education in British-Mandated Palestine was notable, producing a Palestine-Arab population (now largely refugees) which was among the most politically sophisticated in the whole region. Throughout the whole Arab world, one of the prime goals of nationalist educational policy has been to make Arabic the basic language and the basis of culture.

Nevertheless, the general picture is still one of illiteracy to the order of 75 per cent., and of a lack of modern technological skills that in itself retards rapid economic development. The constant and rapid increase in population imposes a severe burden on school-building programmes. There is a grim race even to keep abreast of this increase, let alone achieve the general goal of free public education for all at primary —and ultimately higher—levels. In addition, there are insufficient qualified teachers: since 1936 most Arab countries have had to employ Egyptian staff in increasing numbers, and/or Palestinian and Syrian graduates.

An immediate measure of modern nationalist governments has been the reform and redistribution of land tenure. In Tunisia, where one-quarter of the cultivated land was owned by Europeans before independence, the Government is buying up these estates as the European (mainly French) population dwindles, and will redistribute the acreage to landless peasants. In Algeria, to this day, one-third of all cultivated land is owned by some 21,000 Europeans; 6 million Moslems (i.e. Arab-Algerians) live on the rest, 3 million being landless with work for only a few days every year. In Egypt, before the 1952 revolution, some 2,000 landowners (out of 2·7 million) held one-fifth of all the cultivated land. This was confiscated against State bonds in compensation, and redistributed to some 1·2 million peasants (together with a law fixing land rents, which relieved tenant-farmers of some £40 million each year). An early measure by the

Iraqi revolutionary régime was similar confiscation of the great sheikhly tribal estates: in pre-1958 Iraq (under the Nuri Government), 96 per cent. of the rural population owned no land whatsoever. Soon after the 1958 union with Egypt, land reform was also begun in Syria. Reforms have not yet been carried out in Lebanon, where half the cultivated acreage is in the hands of some 200 great landowners with considerable political power.

The *economic* effect of land reform, however, is necessarily limited. It redistributes political power, and affords a valuable access of dignity to profoundly depressed peasants. In the case of Iraq, redistribution is so radical—because previous tenure was so thoroughly feudal—that the socio-economic effects will be truly revolutionary. But reform, by itself, cannot solve rural over-population; and because the new proprietors are unskilled in modern agriculture, their organization into compulsory co-operatives, farming by uniform crop-belts embracing many small parcels, is essential. It is, indeed, quite clear that agricultural co-operatives need to be extended over virtually all Arab cultivation, as the only effective way of providing credit for seed, fertilizer and machinery; of maintaining high productivity against the fragmentation of holdings; and of ensuring efficient marketing. This is the pronounced aim in Egypt, Syria, Iraq and Tunisia. Arab nationalists have a deep-seated antipathy to the Communist idea of collectives; co-operation is the favoured alternative, to be extended by persuasion.

The far greater problem, however, is to increase the cultivated acreage to the very maximum consistent with water supply. Direct rainfall offers only limited opportunities, and in many areas—for example, in parts of Morocco—it varies so widely from year to year as to make permanent culture very difficult. There are, broadly, four great potential systems of water supply in the Arab world: the Atlas-Aurès Mountains in the Maghrib; the Nile waters for Egypt and the Sudan; the Jordan Valley system, involving Lebanon, Syria, Jordan and Israel; and the Tigris-Euphrates system on the great plain of Iraq, also affecting northern Syria. It must be accounted one of the tragedies of the mid-twentieth-century Arab world that proper, *integrated* exploitation of these water systems has not been pursued earlier and urgently.

Many exploitation schemes in individual countries are, however, under construction. Some of the most important include the controversial High Dam at Aswan in Upper Egypt. This mammoth undertaking, designed to store Nile flood-waters, will provide irrigation for a further 1 to 2 million acres (present area, 6 million). In the Sudan, opportunities to increase the cultivated area are much greater. The new Manaqil Canal will irrigate 600,000 more acres; the projected Roseires Dam a further 3 million acres (1955 total irrigated area, 6 million acres). Syrian irrigation projects could increase the cultivated area by some 50 per cent. Iraq's millennial irrigation system, wrecked by the thirteenth-century Mongol invasion, is now being restored by dams and flood-control barrages, and irrigated acreage could be increased by 55 per cent. The potential of the Jordan Valley, however, is held up by the conflict with Israel. Proper use of the Jordan water system could provide new land for some 160,000

Jordanians (but not, as is often presumed, for all her 500,000 Palestine refugees).

The extent to which these irrigation projects could "solve" Arab population problems varies considerably from country to country, and is by no means as hopeful as might appear. For example, population increase in Algeria makes it doubtful that even a 100 per cent. increase in cultivated area, equably distributed and fully exploited, could prove sufficient. In Egypt, the annual population increase of over 500,000 cannot possibly be met by the High Dam's future addition to the irrigated area; indeed, by the time this addition is effected, it will only just restore the present ratio of population to cultivated land. In degree, this is the prospect throughout the area. And it predicates that the only complete answer is massive industrialization as well, in the hope that a standard of living can be reached, despite the population-explosion, that will then produce the classic relative decrease in birth-rate experienced in the West.

This, however, is merely to state the ideal. Industrialization requires power; the hydro-electric power schemes now in construction (like that embodied in the High Dam) demand vast capital investment; and it is the usual characteristic of underdeveloped areas that Arab rates of internal capital formation are low. Of the countries capable of industrialization, Iraq, with its own oil income, is best placed; an independent Algeria, sharing in the wealth of Saharan oil and natural gas, would also be favourably placed. Otherwise, capital must come from abroad, and from those Arab oil-producing territories in the Persian Gulf that have very small populations and enormous capital surpluses (notably Kuwait, pop. 200,000, annual oil income over £100 million).

Political Institutions

The Arab world that is in the throes of external crisis, and is confronted by these grave economic problems, is also caught in a major internal political revolution. As with the economic struggle, there is no clear-cut choice of exemplary political institutions. Among the most difficult lessons to be learned from Afro-Asian events in the last decade is the manifest evidence that the traditional Western-liberal assumption of a clear choice of "democracy" or "Communism" is a major over-simplification. By "democracy" has always been meant Western-style party-parliamentary government. Egypt, the Sudan, Syria, Iraq, Pakistan, Ghana, Burma and other Afro-Arab-Asian countries did once possess quite sound constitutions following this Western model. In the Arab world, as in Africa and Asia proper, the overwhelming legacy of political conviction among educated people has been that of Western democracy, imbibed in Western or Western-influenced schools and colleges. In revolution after revolution by modern nationalist movements, democracy of this kind has been a fundamental goal, in the revolution led by Nasser no less than in others.

Yet the sombre fact is that Western-style parliamentary democracy has increasingly broken down, and has disappeared or been suspended, all over this great region. In regard to the Arab world, perhaps the greatest and most recent shock to the traditional liberal hope was the coup by Army officers in the Sudan. At the time of writing, the pattern of Arab political institutions can be very briefly described as follows:

Morocco: King Mohammed V's 1958 Royal Charter stipulated that the monarch should retain legislative power. Municipal and rural district councils are to be elected; these will send representatives to a National Assembly that will vote on the Budget, but will otherwise be consultative only; ultimately, at a date not defined, the Assembly will be elected by universal franchise.

Algeria: at the time of writing, Algeria remains French; its political institutions are scarcely relevant, therefore, to this enquiry.

Tunisia: President Bourguiba was elected, unopposed, in November, 1959. He exercises extremely strong powers, and freedom of the press is drastically curtailed. The constitution under preparation will probably provide for a strong, popularly elected, fixed-term executive, and a national assembly whose effective powers, judging by current conditions, will be very limited.

Libya: King Idris I legislates largely by royal decree, though there is a Parliament and there have been two general elections. The contest between Palace and Parliament is almost inevitable at this extremely youthful stage.

United Arab Republic: political parties are banned; the press is controlled; President Nasser and his Ministers rule without legislative restraint, though there is evidence that the judiciary retains considerable independence. In July, 1959, elections were held to choose village, district and provincial committees of the non-party "National Union" (open to all adults). An Assembly for Egypt and Syria will be appointed by the

President; at a later stage, Deputies will be elected in normal constituencies, but will have consultative powers only for an indeterminate "transition period".

The Sudan: since November, 1958, a junta of Army officers has governed by decree, the parliamentary constitution being suspended and parties banned. Premier General Abboud's intentions for the political future are not clear, but he has intimated that, in his opinion, the Sudan is "not ready for Western democracy".

Jordan: the Cabinet elected by the first Jordanian Parliament, returned at genuinely free elections in October, 1956, was dismissed by King Hussein in April, 1957. After more than a year of martial law, political activity is restricted to those figures and parties approved by the King, who relies on an Army purged of Arab-nationalist officers, and especially on its loyal Bedouin core.

Lebanon: the last, manipulated, election was in 1957. In the aftermath of civil war, an impartial President (General Chehab) acts as umpire over a Cabinet drawn from both sides of the conflict. New elections to Parliament must await a general access of confidence and calm.

Iraq: since the July, 1958, revolution, Brigadier-General Kassem has been Prime Minister. In January, 1960, he approved the licensing for political activity of three Communist or Communist-dominated parties (including a Kurdish group) and the National Democratic Party. Elections for a new parliament have been promised for July, 1960, but the demoralization of non-Communists, and general instability, make the event, and certainly the outcome, doubtful.

Saudi Arabia: a supreme Islamic monarchy without legislature, advised by a Council of Ministers composed of members of the royal family; the sole judiciary is the Islamic (puritanical Wahabi sect) hierarchy.

Other Arab countries, including Yemen, are highly autocratic, under dynastic potentates with or without British treaty-supervision. In short, nowhere in the entire Arab world can it be said that democracy, according to Western precepts and practices, now functions. It would be a singular error, however, to perpetuate earlier assumptions that this absence of democracy is caused by sheer personal power-ambition —or, for that matter, by any inherent and particular "defect" in Arabs. The problem is by no means so simple, nor is the authoritarian nationalist leadership that of mere egoism. There is a growing feeling that the Western system of democracy, based on free party-political activity, cannot simply be transplanted into Arab society; that earlier attempts to emulate Western practice failed not only because of the character of political leadership, but because the conditions of Arab society are so very different from those in which Western democracy functions.

Having noted this doubt, it must then be said that those who profess it have not yet offered either a clear explanation of it or a coherent new philosophy of democracy. In part, this weakness must again be attributed to the past unhealthy preoccupation with external issues and crises; in part to the fact that many of the doubters are not well-educated intellectuals but only moderately educated officer-activists; in part to the absence of any foreign (non-Communist) alternative system as a guide; and in part to the simple fact that dictators are under no special provocation to defend and therefore elaborate their doubts. Trenchant examination of the actual course of Arab politics, however, and equally trenchant discussion with the doubters can yield a tentative set of conclusions.

The overwhelming majority of any potential Arab electorate is illiterate (Lebanon being the only exception); extremely poor; and without a consciousness of being part of a nation-*state*, as have Western citizens. Nor do most Arabs have any social organization helping to give them this sense of national citizenship. As between Ottoman Turkish rule (or separate local tribal authority) and the system of government that developed in Europe during the same centuries, there can be little useful comparison. Neither in terms of parliament or local self-government, nor in terms of guilds, corporations, and other functional bodies, nor in terms of Church, has the Arab world had those steadily evolving conceptual and functional bonds between the individual and his community that proved so vital in the rise of Western democracy. What happened was rather that the *skeleton* of the Western nation-state, the *textbook* constitution and the spirit and principles of Western democracy, were imported into a politically inert society by its small educated minority. Inside this skeletal structure, and below this educated minority, there still lives a peasant majority in a genuine social void. The bonds of authority and obligation which the Arab peasant recognizes are those of his family head (a family may comprise thousands), his relatives, his local *ulema* (priest, but with no hierarchy above him), and his landlord. If he is a Moslem, he is conscious of being a member of the *umma*, or

Moslem community. But while he may generally venerate such Islamic dignitaries as the Sheikh of El-Azhar University or King Saud, keeper of the Holy Cities, not even in his religious devotion and observances is there a functional hierarchy that provides him with a sense of active participation in a larger community.

The rise of nationalism, and of the idea that progress is possible, has most certainly added to the Arab peasant's horizon. He admires and supports a leader like Bourguiba, Nasser or Kassem—but as his *batal*, his champion, rather than as the head of a democratic nation-state of which he, the peasant, is an obliging and obliged citizen. Nationalism has introduced him to *an* idea of democracy that so far concerns dignity and greater material prosperity rather than responsibility in government. Indeed, it could be said that he would not entirely welcome the idea of his leader being "government"—in the Western sense—because government is to him a negative concept connoting a man who comes to collect taxes and issue orders.

It is, then, on such an electorate that a model Western democracy, based on political parties contesting for votes and then competing for government, would have to rest at present. But the system, from the civil service through the legislature and to the actual parties, must be operated by the educated minority. That minority has a standard of living which it wishes to maintain, if not improve; and such maintenance, let alone improvement, involves a very profound clash with the economic needs of the masses. It may involve issues of land tenure, in the reform of which the minority must legislate against itself; or the question of whether foreign currency shall be used for cars and refrigerators or for capital development goods. The political parties cannot be broadly and nationally representative in their active membership and leadership. They cannot "divide" according to "class", in the Western sense, because there are no such divisions. Division according to existing income strata would obstruct the most elementary national progress and unity. The parties tend to represent traditional forces (religion, tribe, language, section); coteries of influential men; and intellectual splinter groups whose theories are of doubtful utility in formulating practical national policy. Because they are truly minority parties in a poor society of strong family ties, patronage plays an undue role in their contest for power. Even those great nationalist parties that assume majority power in a newly sovereign country tend to reveal themselves, in the subsequent stress of legislative responsibility, as amalgams of many incompatible interests—landlord and peasant, magnate and worker, prince and intellectual. Their unity during the drive for freedom gravely diminishes once freedom is attained.

Against this condition of society, and the paramount need for a strong, stable, incorruptible executive to carry out development programmes, the viability of Western-style democracy can only be highly questionable. Practical experience of trying to operate party-parliamentary democracy has led to great doubt as to its very suitability. No one has any "blueprint" as an alternative. A scene illustrative of this search is that of an Arab officer-nationalist, surrounded by Western textbooks on political theory and practice, who pushes them aside and says, "I can find no guidance from these for our own problems." He *is* imbued with fundamentally democratic convictions in the widest sense: his problem is to translate them into a steadily developing system of politics that will provide for stable executive government, internal order and national unity, and the practice of democratic responsibility by the peasant, until something more closely resembling a Western society can more feasibly operate what is meant by democracy in the West.

Broadly, the tentative new approaches to ultimate democracy in the Arab world involve three ideas. The minimal one is that the executive must be popularly elected for a fixed term, and must not be in constant jeopardy from a "fickle" party-based parliament. In short, the British constitutional system is widely deemed the least suitable of all. A second idea is that democracy can only develop from the bottom, not from the top; from a newly articulate peasantry that has learned what the rights and obediences of democracy involve. The priority laid down in the Moroccan Royal Charter illustrates this approach: first, elections to municipal and rural-district councils; then, at a later stage, representation from these councils to a purely consultative national assembly; and then—and only then—election of parliamentary representatives by adult franchise in constituencies.

The implication in this approach is that, until the peasant majority of the electorate has gone through some initial "training school" of democracy in local circles of representation that it can understand, freedom of national political parties—in the full, Western sense—is undesirable and, in fact, will not produce democracy. Always, in the contemporary clamour of doubt, the emphasis is on the dangers and impossibilities of democracy *based on parties*. It must indeed be noted that this derives partly from the impatience of nationalist army officers with the "ditherings and bickerings" of civilian "politicians" in times that demand such forthright progress. But even among civilian intellectuals there is growing doubt about the role of parties.

The third and most radical, most unprecedented, approach is that of the oldest nationalist officer-dictatorship—President Nasser and his colleagues. Nasser has never quite abandoned his original, highly optimistic ideal of a nation, liberated from the twin shackles of "imperialism" and internal exploitation, moving, united and self-restrained, towards the goal of a more equable and prosperous society. He admits that he had his roseate vision before the 1952 coup, and was subsequently gravely disillusioned by the continuing disunity of old parties. Today, his approach is firmly directive, but based on the idea of a non-party consensus of all citizens. To institute the "training-school in democracy" for the mass of illiterate peasants, village committees have been elected, and also district and provincial committees. If these are truly given useful and tangible functions, it will itself be a great step forward, for, in Egypt and Syria as elsewhere, the masses have not even known the association with government that derives from local responsibility.

The U.A.R. "National Union" predicates that, from these beginnings at the base of the social pyramid, progressive circles of democratic representation can be added up towards the executive, going through a consultative legislative phase until, at some undefined later date, new and representative parties will emerge. Meanwhile, there is no doubt that the executive will remain strong; its popularity will be proven only by periodic election; and those elections will be democratic only if a reasonable climate of debate, freedom of candidature, and secret voting are permitted.

In conclusion, it can be predicted that no new, "gradualist" approach to genuine democracy can succeed unless the executive is enlightened, capable of tolerating and heeding criticism in the press and elsewhere, and able to win the confidence of the Western-inspired educated minority. This last element is surely vital. The personal ambitions, the special interests, the sincere desire to contribute ideas and energies of the educated minority of the Arab world must be fully harnessed to government and development. Broad external-nationalist slogans will not satisfy this intelligentsia; the sterility of a controlled press and the prohibition of political controversy will not stimulate that very intellectual vitality on which Arab civilization depends. What Arab leaders who doubt the present suitability of Western democracy are saying is that they want all these elements, but not via political parties and a powerful, party-based legislature. They must therefore find new ways of associating the precious minority of educated brains and skilled energies with leadership and national progress. They must constantly remind themselves that, even assuming they can survive a continued *crise de confiance* with the intelligentsia, little will have been gained if a new, democratically trained peasantry emerges from the villages into an urban atmosphere that is stagnant and sterile from political and intellectual repression.

The search for new forms of Afro-Arab-Asian democracy continues, and the above can only be a highly tentative judgement. As this chapter is written, it is clear that Arab nationalism has entered a new phase of conflict—against internal Communism. The Arab Communist is not necessarily a slavish imitator of the Soviet political system, or—more particularly— of the Chinese experiment with the Commune. But it seems quite safe to predict that the rise to power of an Arab Communist Party would result in draconian (and, if events in Iraq are an index, brutal) forms of political repression unlike anything so far witnessed even under outright officer-nationalist dictatorship. The real internal struggle in the Arab world in the next decade will be determined by the extent to which non-Communist nationalist leadership—activist and intellectual —can achieve rapidly maturing new political institutions as well as economic progress, in competition with the Sino-Soviet example. That example is very much more relevant to Arab conditions than the West's.

In short, it is salutary for the Westerner to reflect that the Soviet Union and China can both pose as external "friends" *and* offer the Arabs a striking internal example. The West cannot do the latter, not in the sense of simply offering Western constitutions ready made; and it has largely been deprived, by *its own past policy*, of doing the former. But the West *can* sympathetically assist Arab intellectuals and politicians in their search for a new, *indigenous* democratic ideology and system. Academic research is needed on a new premise: that the idealized Western constitution may *not* be the only form of democracy. At the same time, it is quite clear that a climate of general liberty, during the Arab world's "transition periods", will depend not only on how leadership can deal with internal Communist challenges, but also on the disappearance of obsessions about Western pressure and intrigue. Fear of such pressure—whether real, imagined, or used as an excuse—is a major obstacle to such a climate, and will continue to be so long as conflict continues on such issues as Algeria, Aden, the Gulf States, and Western bases in the region.

Finally, there is a transparent and urgent need for external capital and technical assistance. The legacy of past years, when such aid from the West was heavily stigmatized by cold-war conditions, will not be quickly overcome. Whether the Sino-Soviet bloc agree or not, Western help should be channelled through the United Nations for the Arab world, as for the rest of the Afro-Asian region.

CHAPTER EIGHT

ARABS AND ISRAEL

MENTION HAS ALREADY been made of the impact
on Arab nationalism, since 1917, of Jewish immigration into Palestine, culminating in Israel's emergence
as a state. Both factors have added to Arab nationalism
an obsessive bitterness and fear such as no other Afro-
Asian movement has experienced, and have profoundly
exacerbated nationalist hostility towards all three
Western Powers. It was a British Government which
issued the Balfour Declaration; and it was under a
British Mandate that immigration was sanctioned
(though later efforts were made to restrict the influx).
The United States supported Jewish immigration from
D.P. camps after World War II and the 1947 U.N.
Partition resolution; and President Truman gave
immediate *de facto* recognition to the state of Israel.
Arab hostility towards France now derives, in addition
to the Algerian war, from her collusion with Israel in
the 1956 Sinai attack.

Events in Palestine have also accelerated the entry
of the Soviet Union into the Arab world as a Middle
Eastern Power, following a calculated change of Soviet
policy from early support for the establishment of
Israel to outright sponsorship of the Arab case against
Israel. Similarly, the Arab-Israeli conflict was the origin
of the Egyptian Government's Czech (i.e. Soviet bloc)
arms agreement of late 1955—the first major Soviet
bloc success of this kind. There is, however, little

doubt that the rise of the Soviet Union as a Power directly involved in Middle Eastern affairs was inevitable; and her entry into the region as another source of arms was also in any case likely. Nevertheless, it was over the future of Palestine that the pace, and the intensive cold-war character, of this trend was made possible. Among the repercussions of this development is the close diplomatic and political connection between the status of Jews in Soviet bloc countries and Soviet-Arab relations. Soviet Communism is hostile to Zionism as an international movement promoting loyalties other than to the states of which Jews are citizens. This hostility, together with local anti-Semitism, creates insecurity for Jews in Soviet bloc countries whom the Israeli Government wishes to bring to Israel. Equally, any Soviet decision to permit such emigration must be weighed against the risks of injuring Soviet-Arab relations, since one of the prime Arab fears is of further expansionism following Jewish immigration into the small Israeli State.

The role of Palestine in Soviet policy has merely added new power-political factors to a dispute already enmeshed in world power politics. The dictates of British and French strategic and commercial interests in the Arab world, and of American oil interests, have already put these three Western Powers in a dilemma in their policies towards Zionism. The French Government of M. Mollet decided in 1956 that an Israeli attack against Egypt—to help bring about the downfall of President Nasser—was necessary in view of Egypt's support for the Algerian nationalists. On the other hand, the British Government of Sir Anthony Eden—who was a trained Arabist—did not wish to be publicly connected with the Israeli attack. In general, Western governments were torn between the necessity of maintaining relations with Arabs and pressures from their own public opinion in support of Jewish immigration into Palestine. At the critical stage immediately after World War II, a further factor was reluctance to admit Jewish displaced persons, survivors of the Nazi genocide of 6 million Jews, into *Western* countries. There was also the opposition of Zionist organizations to any such admission, lest it should detract from their goal of resurrecting a strong, well-populated Jewish nation-state in Palestine. Once that State had been proclaimed and endorsed by the U.S. Government, the Western dilemma became extremely difficult to solve. It could be seen in the 1950 Tripartite Declaration (America, Britain and France), which sought to guarantee the Armistice *status quo* in Palestine pending a peace settlement, and to ensure a balance of arms supplies as between Israel and the Arab States. This Declaration, however, was feasible only so long as the Soviet Union remained uninterested. It was further nullified by Anglo-French actions, in contact with the Israeli Government, in the Sinai-Suez War.

The sources of international support for the Zionist yearning (by no means unanimous among Jews) to return to a homeland claimed as Jewish for some 2,000 years have been varied. The ideas and hopes behind this support have necessarily suffered in the outcome of the struggle. In the Western world there were many—including key British political leaders between 1900 and 1917—whose religious sentiments favoured the Zionist dream of a Holy Land Jewish homeland. An additional Zionist argument of considerable power was that a strong Jewish community in Palestine could safeguard the Holy Places for non-Moslem faiths, and could provide Britain with a vigorous, friendly flanking power near the Suez Canal. The concept of a dynamic, progressive Jewish community in Palestine, injecting Western ideas of democracy into a decadent Arab world, was also a prime source of liberal international support. The socialist aims of Zionism made this concept particularly attractive to British socialists. Finally, there was very widespread humanitarian sympathy for the victims of the disease of anti-Semitism, reaching its zenith immediately after World War II when the full horror of the Nazi genocide became known. A subconscious sense of guilt towards Jews among very many Christians contributed to the success of Zionist efforts.

These positive ideas and hopes were matched by the general lack of information about Arabs, and about Palestine, that has conditioned so much of the Western approach to the Arab world in this century. Many of the myths and fallacies described in an earlier chapter were involved. The Zionist claim that Palestine had always been Jewish was made easier by a very widespread belief that the territory was certainly not an Arab land; that such Arabs as could be found in it were nomads, neither cultivating nor residing. In fact, of some 640,000 Arabs (Moslem and Christian) in Palestine in 1917, only 10 per cent. were nomads, the remainder being two-thirds settled peasants and one-third urban inhabitants. Again, the existence of Arab national sentiment was little appreciated. The peace settlements after World War I, confirming the detachment of Palestine from Greater Syria as a British

Mandate pledged to the Jewish National Home, were concluded without any enquiry among the inhabitants or their neighbours. The only investigating team that went out to the area was that of the American Commissioners, whose report—confirming the strongest antipathy to Zionism, and the existence of an Arab national movement—was not considered by the Versailles Powers. It was only later made public at the instance of one of the Commissioners.

The result was tragic but inevitable. The strategic, political and social hopes held by Western supporters of Zionism were all (predictably) confounded by Arab hostility. The Mandate principle of self-determination for indigenous inhabitants could not be reconciled with the continuous immigration of aliens whose leaders sought an exclusively Jewish-led state. The strategic hope of a "pro-British" Israel guarding the eastern flank of the Suez Canal has recurred intermittently, but could not be consolidated by any British Government for fear of arousing still greater Arab anger outside Palestine. The political and social dream—shared by many Jews—of a dynamic Jewish example to Arabs depended entirely on harmonious relations and free intercourse between the Arab States and Israel. The very reverse has transpired, and many entirely meritorious potential examples in Israeli institutions—for example, the Histadruth comprehensive labour federation—are stigmatized because they are Zionist. The aim of protecting the Holy Places has been confounded not only by the division of Palestine, but by Zionist refusal to consider the internationalization of Jerusalem. Finally, the humanitarian impulse that led to such widespread international support for the resettlement of Jewish refugees has helped to create a conflict involving the uprooting and exile of nearly 1 million Arabs.

As against these grave failures, however, there is the establishment in Palestine of a dynamic, remarkably progressive State whose Jewish population now stands at nearly 2 million—as against 55,000 in 1917. The domestic achievements of Israel, while they have proved possible only with a continuous capital import from world Jewry and other sources, totalling some £1,000 million since 1949, testify to the spirit and energies of its citizens. But their lives, and this massive investment, must stand in continuous—and probably increasing—jeopardy so long as Arabs have cause to fear what they regard as an alien, messianic expansionism in their homeland. It is Israel's dilemma that the past record and continuing ideology of Zionism *ipso facto* suggest, not peace, but grave danger to her Arab neighbours. To a past that can only be interpreted by Arabs as expansionism and the expulsion of Arabs is added a future in which the State of Israel is dedicated in law to the mission of ingathering the rest of the world's Jews—numbering over 10 million. The immediate goals of Israel's leadership envisage a population of at least 4 millions. This suggests to Arabs a permanent umbilical cord of finance, propaganda and diplomatic "intrigue" between Israel, world Jewry and the Powers, in order to support such a population. The official publications of Israel include such inevitably provocative references as that "the establishment of the State in no way derogates from the scope of historical Eretz Israel" (the much larger ancient Israel). In attacks like that in Sinai, Israeli officials claimed that the Peninsula was not part of "Egypt proper", and spoke of "liberating the homeland". Given the past, the Arab conclusion is virtually inevitable, *whether right or wrong in fact*.

How Israel can change this fearful picture—which provokes an Arab hostility that offers Israelis no less fearful a future—is among the greatest questions confronting the Arab world in this new decade. That the initiative must come from Israel seems an obvious conclusion from the last decade of explosive *impasse*.

CHAPTER NINE

ARAB UNION

THE THEME AND the urge of Arab unity, of an "Arabism", has obtruded through much of the history related in earlier chapters. It was noted how the permanent legacy of a common Arabization—in language, culture, and customs—fused in the nineteenth and twentieth centuries with the Western idea of nationhood in the nation-state. Even in the 1850s, a few Arab intellectuals conceived of an Arab nation embracing all peoples who spoke Arabic, irrespective of creed. But the general early response to Western ideas was haphazard, and the fusion with the Arab legacy did not in fact mature until (roughly) the 1930s. The reasons have already been mentioned: the early lack of communications either by persons or by printed words between different parts of the Arabized world; Egypt's preoccupation with purely Egyptian nationalism after the British occupation of 1882; the continuance of a different, Turkish oppressor in the Arab East; the post-Versailles dismemberment of that Arab East into several sovereignties, each with rising local vested interests in division.

But beneath these events, and despite their impact, there persisted and grew a sense of "Arabism". In Egypt, and in all other parts of the Arab world, Arabic increasingly became the medium used for rapidly developing press, publishing and educational facilities. In the twentieth century, intercommunications of every kind within this world grew very quickly. The latent impulse towards an Arab nationalism, below what the outside world tended to see as "Syrian" or "Egyptian" nationalism, was quickened after World War I both by political events and by ideological influence. The struggle against the Western Powers across the whole region, from Morocco to Iraq, and the common anger and fear over Palestine (not, however, so strong in the Maghrib), contributed, as we have seen. But there was also a continuing search among political thinkers and intellectuals for a viable, an indigenous equivalent to the Western concept of nationhood—and this search now encompassed an ever-wider circle of educated men and women in ever-greater contact with each other. New, more powerful ideological influences circulated among them from West and East: notably, the German mystical idea of the *Volk* or "people", and the rise of modern nationalism in an India where there was not one but 200 languages.

The result may be seen in the very Arabic word that was increasingly used to denote nationalism. Until the 1930s, the prevailing term was *wataniyya*—love of the place of one's birth or dwelling. The link with the French *nationalité* is clear—combining the concepts of legal (or territorial) identity and social (or political) identity. From the 1930s forward, however, a new term came into Arabic usage: *qaumiyya*. The *qaum* was the "folk" community of the old Arab tribes, a community to which the individual owed allegiance no matter where he was. His *qaumiyya* transcended place, whether of birth or of dwelling. In the rise of the phrase *qaumiyya arabiyya*—"Arab peoplehood"—may be seen the nationalist search for an identity between all who were Arab, irrespective of whether they were citizens of, say, an Iraqi or a Jordanian state. Today, the phrase may be said to be universal for "Arab nationalism", conveying at once an idea to which every person who speaks Arabic and lives in the cultural heritage of Arabization can respond. It transcends frontiers as the world sees them on the map of the region; it transcends religion (the Christian Arab can feel the same response). It provokes a continuous psychological stress between the citizen in his legally constituted state and this wider community of Arabs of which he feels himself a part.

But the translation of this emotive concept into concrete, constitutional Arab unity will not be easy. Before the major "Young Arab" revolution of the 1950s, the response of the older leadership to this rising demand was limited to the formation of the Arab League in 1945. This is an association between Arab states "to strengthen the ties between [them], to co-ordinate their political programmes in such a way as to effect real collaboration between them", *and*, however, "to preserve their independence and sovereignty". How far *qaumiyya arabiyya* has advanced since then may be judged by references in the documents creating the union of Egypt and Syria in the United Arab Republic:

"This unity which is the fruit of Arab nationalism is the Arabs' path to sovereignty and freedom . . . to take this unity . . . out of the circle of wishes and aspirations to where it can be converted into a reality . . . the new Republic shall have one flag, one army, one people [who] are part of the Arab Nation. . . ."

The formation of this, the first concrete expression

of the dream of Arab unity, caused consternation among rulers and leaders of the older epoch. Within three weeks it provoked the proclamation of a Hashemite union between the related dynasties of Iraq and Jordan, while King Saud of Saudi Arabia attempted to disrupt the Egyptian-Syrian union. The fears of conservative leaders in Lebanon were described in an earlier chapter. The union prompted the Iraqi Premier, Nuri es-Said, to plan an invasion of Syria in June, 1958, in order to detach Iraq's neighbour from Egypt. Opposition, or obstacles, to organic Arab unity, however, must not be considered as solely between the *ancien régime* and Young Arabism. There do exist strong retarding forces, and local separatisms, throughout the Arab world; and these will persist in many respects even after the fundamental struggle between two leadership-epochs has ended. The outcome is difficult to predict, but a number of governing factors can be seen.

The Great Powers

Until World War II, it was held to be in the interests of Britain and France in no way to favour or promote close unity between the various constituent parts of the Arab world: many of the existing divisions in the Arab east were imposed by Britain and France after World War I. In the Arab west (the *Maghrib*), it was impossible for France to envisage any form of union between the three major territories—Morocco, Algeria and Tunisia—save as it might facilitate French control and administration. This policy has not, to date, been changed. The loss to independence of Morocco and Tunisia has served only to underline it in respect of Algeria.

In British policy, Egypt and the Sudan were regarded as necessarily separate entities, and their closer unity with Eastern Arab countries was in no way envisaged. By the advent of World War II, however, it was clear that the general impulse towards unity within nationalism, and the strong appeal exercised by the Axis Powers, required some adjustment of attitudes. During the war, Britain twice issued declarations favouring the goal of Arab unity, and accordingly welcomed the formation of the Arab League. Many Arabists in official British circles genuinely favoured such unity, and saw no clash with British interests, provided the leadership of the movement remained favourable to Britain. When, however, the leadership was assumed by an intractably independent Egyptian Government, active support was given to those "friends"—notably Nuri es-Said and King Hussein—who might be able to lead a counter-movement of unity, closely associated with Britain, in the Arab East. The collapse in 1958 of this policy—with which the United States had also by then become wholly identified—has not yet led to any clear further readjustment, either by Britain or the United States. But the indications are that both Powers now recognize that the movement, under whatever leadership, cannot be opposed.

The policies of the Soviet Union have followed a similar pattern. During the 1950s, while the Young Arab movement was actively in conflict with the Western Powers, Russia strongly supported the ideal of unity. The short-term hope was that such support would increase Soviet prestige. The long-term objective was that Arab Communist Parties might then capitalize this prestige and secure increasing actual power from within the nationalist movement. Between 1957 and 1959, however, it evidently became apparent to the Soviet Union, and the Arab Communists, that President Nasser's neutralism would not admit of local Communist activity. Towards the end of 1958, it was decided that the overall nationalist movement as led by Nasser must be broken up—above all by preventing any union between revolutionary Iraq and the United Arab Republic, and by creating in Iraq a political base from which to detach Syria from Egypt. Future Soviet policy will no doubt be adjusted according to the opportunities that present themselves.

The Maghrib

In the likely evolution of Arab union, the character of the *Maghrib* or Arab West, strongly suggests a regional unit of its own within the Arab world. Considerably isolated from the East by distance and desert, its physical environment is unitary. It contains cultural elements, perhaps especially the Berber strains, whose lesser Arabization, and historic resistance to centralized authority, make a Maghribian unit more likely than an organic merger of these countries with the rest of the Arab world. A glimpse of this likely course may be seen in the Resolution of the Tangier Conference of April, 1958, which spoke of "the will of the peoples of the Arab Maghrib . . . for [federal] union . . .". At the same time, there *is* a growing sense of commonalty with the rest of the Arab world in Morocco, Algeria, and Tunisia. In 1958, both Morocco and Tunisia joined the Arab League, while the Algerian nationalists have long had close, though not servile, relations with Egypt and other eastern nationalist régimes. In 1959 the Arab League met for the first time at Casablanca.

Libya, with a small population and very youthful as a political entity, is a member of the Arab League, but the precise direction of her Arab ties is unpredictable. King Idris I, however, formally accepted the Tangier Resolution, and it may not be surprising to see a progressive trend towards the Maghrib by this small bridge-country, rather than towards the Egyptian giant to the east.

Egypt and the Sudan

Their vital common interest in the Nile waters by itself creates a permanent bond between Egypt and the Sudan, although agreement on the distribution of those waters (1959) was not easy. Egyptian fear of foreign pressure via the Sudan's higher position on the Nile was alleviated by the Sudanese military coup of 1958. The two countries are natural partners, and ever-closer links may be expected. The Sudan, however, includes a southern region whose long isolation from the impact of Arabization makes for tensions, and these would probably increase over any trend towards a union in which southern Sudanese—at this stage of their development—might fear Egyptian domination.

Egypt and the Arab East

Egypt's resumption of an active, leading role in Arab politics is recent. But it is a resumption, and it follows a long period in which she had held such a role in Arab cultural, educational, informational and technological developments. Concern over events beyond her eastern frontiers has been a recurring feature of Egypt's history. It is complemented by a considerable appreciation in the Arab East that Egypt is a vital source of Arab-world strength—indeed, has repeatedly been a "key" to foreign conquest of the region. To modern Arab nationalists, Nasser's assertion of political leadership, far from being the "non-Arab intrusion" so widely adjudged in the Western world, was hailed as a "return".

Nevertheless, a monolithic centrally controlled or directed Arab union, whether based on Egypt or on any other large country, is most unlikely. There are grounds for believing that the Egyptian-Syrian union is not likely to be the model for wider unity. Carried out in haste and fear, it was a total merger by Syrian request, and has tended to make Egyptian leadership dominant in the smaller Syrian Region, in which all party-political activity was suspended. After the first electrified wave of enthusiasm, Nasser's own misgivings about the additional responsibility were matched by a certain doubt elsewhere in the area—even among ardent nationalists—whether they should join such a merger. The doubt was and is not of President Nasser as such, but of a wider union under a political system whose very lack of democratic activity would make reasonable regional autonomy difficult. Put in another way, the fear is not simply of Egyptian dictatorship *versus* separate democracy, for it is increasingly appreciated (as discussed in an earlier chapter) that Arab society needs a strong executive not jeopardized by party strife in parliament. The issue is seen rather as between a strong executive largely based in Cairo and a local (i.e. Iraqi) executive.

In short, one of the major obstacles, or retarding factors, in the orderly and comfortable evolution of Arab union is precisely that lack of a coherent, progressive approach to democracy already discussed. It is all too correct to observe that modern Arab nationalism has concentrated its energies and enthusiasms on the moral concept of union, but not on the hard, cold problems of constitutional forms and political institutions. As a result, and given the inevitable stature and power of Egypt, it could be argued that the early draconian character of the union with Syria was ultimately unfortunate. It accelerated the popular urge towards union, but its unitary form set up apprehensions among other leaders. That the Communist Parties were able to benefit from these stresses there can be little doubt. The union has since been somewhat decentralized, but the issue of a degree of autonomy remains.

The inadequate development of political institutions suitable to Arab union, however, is only one among several serious problems.

Minorities

In a number of important Arab countries, there exist minorities or key cultural groups whose attitudes towards Arab union cannot be disregarded by its exponents. The apprehensions of Lebanese Christians have already been cited: they will continue so long as the role of Moslem communal sentiment in *qaumiyya* is unclear. In northern Iraq, there is a large Kurdish community, over 800,000 strong—historically separatist, with a non-Arabic dialect, and strongly wooed by a Kurdish nationalist campaign from Soviet Armenia (Kurds live in Persia, Iraq, Syria, Turkey, and Armenia). The tribes of southern Sudan have not been Arabized, and tend to resist such influence. Factors of this kind will play a part in the evolution of Arab unity, to some degree governing the closeness of union of the countries concerned with other Arab countries.

Oil

The concept of the regional use of resources, given powerful impetus by the Allied supply system during World War II, increasingly infuses the search for Arab unity. Not unnaturally, it raises the question of oil wealth. This takes two forms. Where oil income is in the hands of highly autocratic and conservative rulers, fear of union involves fear for the royal or sheikhly purse; and this despite the fact that *qaumiyya arabiyya* can indeed move rulers in whom feeling for Arab tradition (tribal lineage from the early Arabian conquerors, etc.) is strong. Iraq and Kuwait are in different categories: the former because oil income is administered genuinely on behalf of the national economy and development and is wholly absorbed by such development; the latter because, even after massive and ultra-modern public investment, the Sheikh has enormous annual surpluses which at present go largely to the City of London for investment.

The picture of "haves and have-nots" in Arab oil is thus often over-simplified. Of all Arab countries enjoying oil income only Kuwait, with its tiny population, can "help" other Arab economies in the sense of a major diversion of income. A revolution resulting in the union of Saudi Arabia with some other Arab country, for example, would of itself release a surge of popular expectation that, at last, Saudi oil revenues would be used for the benefit of the people of Saudi Arabia. The diversion of Saudi oil wealth to some other treasury would soon provoke strong reaction. The same would be true of Iraq, and to an even greater extent because Iraqi oil income is already devoted to national development. Thus, an Egyptian leader promoting union with Iraq in order to divert Iraqi oil revenues to Egypt would be short-sighted to the point of lunacy. It was significant that even the Ba'ath Party in Iraq—promoting union with the U.A.R. against Nasser's wishes—stipulated that the existing law allocating 70 per cent. of oil revenue to Iraqi development projects should be retained in any such union.

Nevertheless, the distribution of oil wealth does enter into the search for Arab unity. There is a general vein of impatience in Arab nationalism over the level of profits exported by Western exploiting companies (an impatience, however, tempered at official levels by appreciation that all-Arab operation of the oil industry would be technologically impossible and economically dubious, since it might involve not merely oilfield operation, but tankerage and Western marketing as well). The doctrine that all Arab resources, including oil, should be used for the co-ordinated advancement of the whole Arab world has many supporters. Particular impatience is directed against the investment of Kuwaiti capital surpluses outside the region. Both within the Arab League and outside it, the idea of an Arab Development Bank has received growing attention. The general idea would be that both oil-possessor countries and the exploiting companies would lodge 5 per cent. of their revenues in this Bank, from which needy countries could then borrow for approved development schemes.

Other Factors

It need scarcely be mentioned that the ideal of Arab

union comes up against all the usual, normal obstacles in the *status quo* of sovereignty. In a society highly susceptible to mass adulation of one or two major leaders (or "champions"), union inevitably provokes local jealousies and fears for personal prestige. Again, Arab union inevitably challenges commercial and other vested interests developed in the era of many Arab sovereignties. For example, Syrian merchants have not necessarily hailed the radical changes in their fortune or business systems involved in the union with Egypt. The very fact that modern Arab nationalism does not —because it cannot—expropriate the wealth of the commercial community means that a firm source of resistance to union persists below political levels.

Palestine

Finally, it must be noted that the Arab-Israeli conflict intrudes most profoundly into the evolution of Arab unity. It tends to hasten, perhaps too rapidly, the demand for union. The physical "layout" of Israel, which, in the Negev triangle, divides the Arab world by land, is a constant irritant to Arabs. The likelihood of their accepting only the trans-Negev "corridor" between Egypt and Jordan which Israel offers as part of a peace settlement seems remote. At the same time, because Israel fears strong, militarily co-ordinated encirclement, her policy to date has been to threaten war if neighbouring Jordan merges with any other Arab country.

Conclusion

Despite all the above obstacles, the movement towards closer unity is likely to grow, until the world will see a strong, highly co-operative Arab Confederation embracing the entire Arabized region. Within this Confederation (quite possibly a strengthened Arab League), a number of likely "circles of unity" may be foreseen. One will comprise the Maghrib's three countries—or four, with Libya—in a federal union (a federal executive and assembly, with regional administrations). A second federal union is likely to comprise the United Arab Republic (revised), Iraq, Jordan, and possibly Kuwait, Lebanon and the Sudan. The note of question about the last two countries arises from the fact that their internal characteristics and sensitivities may make more likely their initial membership in a third, federative circle. In this group, co-ordinating foreign and defence policies, would be joined the continued separate sovereignties of less advanced states like Saudi Arabia, the Yemen, and the south Arabian and Gulf principalities when they are released from their outmoded treaty ties with Britain.

Given the above catalogue of obstacles to unity, and yet the deeply felt urge towards unity, the continued sardonic scepticism of much Western comment seems inappropriate. It should not be so surprising that Arab leaders profess brotherhood while frequently negating it in their actions. Certainly, it behoves the West to abandon its ancient fears of a strong and united Arab world, and to refrain from those divisive policies which, in the past, have so contributed to tension in the region. The pace, the leadership, and the forms of union are for Arabs to decide. Efforts to dictate or modulate can only lead to unnatural and ill-planned union, serving neither Arabs nor the world as a whole.

CHAPTER TEN

CONCLUSION

IT IS FORTUNATE, but has not always been recognized in the policies of Western Powers, that the cultural, political, and economic ties between the Arab world and the West are infinitely greater than the issues that divide them. As a new decade of very great significance opens in the Arab world, it must be hoped that past errors, and the reactions to them, can fade into history. Forces of all-encompassing change have been released among Arabs, and will increasingly belie many of the traditional views of them as people and as a cultural group. It can surely do nothing but good, however, if the West can set out to come to terms with these human beings very positively, without waiting for the necessity of doing so.

In this new approach, a first premise must indeed be that Arabs are human beings, endowed with all the potential—and all the weaknesses—that characterize the genus. It will surely do us no harm to recognize that we have not always been willing to grant these people membership in the race of which we have long assumed that we are the cultural and technological epitomes. In the very inflexion we have given the word "Arab", and in the use of such terms as "wog" and "gyppo", there lie attitudes that have harmed the Western world's legitimate self-interests quite as much as they have offended and aggrieved a people possessed of great dignity. They are striving to lift themselves in mere decades to a state of political, economic and social development that occupied Western civilization for centuries. It is this monumental, truly historic endeavour that must be our focus—not the poverty, squalor, and violence from which we ourselves are not so very long removed in time.

An essential characteristic of this struggle is the search for a collective personality in a world of such personalities. Because the West has to a great extent passed through this agony—for nationalism is an agony—its continued manifestation in the Arab world and in Afro-Asia is often irritating. Nationalism is, indeed must be, obsolescent in its narrowest political form. But it is surely a valid lesson of modern history—Western history—that it is an experience that cannot simply be by-passed by one group of human beings because they begin it as others seek to end it. And it would be a very grave error of judgement to hold that Arab nationalists are incapable of realizing the obsolescence of their initial search for identity. No less than other modern nationalists of the ex-colonial and ex-tutelary territories of the world, they do believe in the further goals of the United Nations and of genuine international co-operation. But they must be allowed to go through the search for that personality with which they can meet the wider community in full dignity and self-confidence. Their problem is rather unique, in that the ideal expression of this Arab personality does not neatly fit within existing frontiers, or even within natural boundaries—but reaches out across an open region, and seeks to reconcile particularisms with a "peoplehood" whose precise forms are still not clear.

It may be salutary for us, in moments of irritation, to recall that this whole search is the product of the fusion between an idea germinated in Western society and a legacy implanted by the first Arabs. It behoves us, not to hinder the realization of this search, but indeed to help it. For far too long we have been unable to recognize in Arab society ideas which we respect with pride in our own, because we evolved them. The margin of opportunity to come to terms with the Arabs grew exceedingly slender in the 1950s. Perhaps the most charitable view would be that if it did not disappear altogether in a welter of mutual hostility, this was at least as much because of the deep residual faith of Arabs in Western civilization—as distinct from policy—as because of any belated change by our statesmen.

If we can begin to take positive pride in this Arab faith; to recognize the profound bonds we have with them; and to seek to enlarge these bonds in sympathetic co-operation and concrete material assistance, there is no reason why the storms and wounds of recent years should not heal in both worlds. But the residual frictions are many and urgent—from Algeria to Aden, from the tragedy of Palestine to Britain's treaty ties with the Persian Gulf states. None of these issues is insoluble, given a capacity to approach them afresh as problems in human relations. But it will be tragic indeed if a new decade of Arab history must be pocked and scarred with war and crisis while so much poverty awaits alleviation.

History is supposed to assist man to avoid the mistakes which it discloses. It is surely time to profit positively from the lessons which the recent history of the Arab world inexorably offers—no less to the West than to the Arabs themselves.

BIBLIOGRAPHY

Note: the list of works on individual Arab countries is by now so extensive that selection would be extremely difficult. The following short list of books and other references is intended rather as suggested reading on the Arab region and people as a whole, and on such major subjects as may help formation of judgements on Arab ideas and trends. The writer naturally takes full responsibility for parenthetical comment.

Pocket-books

The Arabs in History, Professor Bernard Lewis, Grey Arrow Books, 1958. (A broad, historical survey, especially of the early Arab world, but culminating in the nineteenth- and twentieth-century Western impact.)

The Arabs, Edward Atiyah, Pelican Book No. A350, 1955. (By a distinguished Lebanese-Christian well known in Britain. It is not, of course, up to date but provides a useful complement to Prof. Lewis' work.)

Reference Surveys

The Middle East, Royal Institute of International Affairs, Oxford University Press, Third Edition, 1958. (Undoubtedly the most comprehensive political and economic survey covering Egypt, the Sudan, and the Arab east. Takes an orthodox conservative view of recent nationalism.)

North-west Africa (The Maghrib), ed. Nevill Barbour,

R.I.I.A., Oxford University Press, 1959. (The first Arab West companion volume to the well-known Middle Eastern survey cited above, covering, especially, Morocco, Algeria, Tunisia, and Libya. An excellent contribution.)

Arab Nationalism

The Arab Awakening, George Antonius, Hamish Hamilton, 1955. (The great work by an Arab scholar on the whole rise of nationalism in the nineteenth and twentieth centuries, but only up to the early 1930s.)

Syria and Lebanon, Albert Hourani, R.I.I.A., Oxford University Press, 1946.

Egypt, Tom Little, Benn, 1958.

Revolution in Iraq, "Caractacus", Gollancz, 1959. (An essay in comparative public opinion as it led to the 1958 Iraqi Revolution—what Iraqis really thought. The first analysis of its kind.)

Arab Unity, Fayez Sayegh, Devin-Adair (U.S.A.), 1958. (A systematic analysis of the movement towards Arab Unity up to and inclusive of the formation of the United Arab Republic.)

Articles, etc.

"Philosophy of the Revolution", Gamal Abdel Nasser, may be found in *The Observer*, London, October 10th *et seq.*, 1954, or as an appendix to *The Sphinx Awakes*, Gerald Sparrow, Halc, 1957. (Nasser's short tract loosely setting out his ideas.)

"The Lesson of Palestine", Musa el-Alami, cf. *Middle East Journal* (Washington, D.C.), 1950. (One of the most important expressions of the nationalist reaction to Palestine, elaborating virtually every facet of "Young Arabism", albeit the author was an older-generation Palestine Arab lawyer.)

"Coming to Terms with the Arabs", Michael Ionides, *The Listener*, August 7th, 1958. (A B.B.C. talk on the lessons of the Iraqi Revolution by one of the most perceptive Britons with long working experience in the Middle East.)

"Nasserism", a special issue of the regular monthly magazine, *Middle East Forum*, April, 1959, Alumni Office, American University of Beirut, Lebanon. (A symposium by many distinguished scholars and journalists, both Arab and Western.)

Periodicals

The writer takes the liberty of suggesting that current reading of news from the Arab world will produce the most accurate understanding from the actual despatches of the correspondents of *The Guardian*, *The Times*, *The Observer*, *The Spectator*, and *The Economist* (Middle Eastern Correspondent).

Further Works

In many of the books cited above, but notably in the two reference surveys, excellent detailed bibliographies will guide the interested reader to country-by-country history and analysis, as also to works of economic and other reference.